ERICH VON DÄNIKEN

EVIDENCE

OF THE

GODS

A Visual Tour of Alien Influence in the Ancient World

A division of
The Career Press, Inc.
Pompton Plains, NJ

EVIDENCE OF THE GODS
TRANSLATED BY CHRISTIAN VON ARNIM
EDITED BY DIANA GHAZZAWI
TYPESET BY JEFF PIASKY
Cover design by Howard Grossman/12E Design
Printed in the U.S.A.

To order this title, please call toll-free 1-800-CAREER-1 (NJ and Canada: 201-848-0310) to order using VISA or MasterCard, or for further information on books from Career Press.

The Career Press, Inc.
220 West Parkway, Unit 12
Pompton Plains, NJ 07444
www.careerpress.com
www.newpagebooks.com

Library of Congress Cataloging-in-Publication Data

CIP Available Upon Request.

Contents

Author's Note

Dear Reader,

"I have read all of your books!" I hear that sentence after every lecture or book signing. And when I delve a little deeper, it turns out that "all of your books" really means six to eight titles. In the meantime, I have written 30 books, and only a few enthusiasts have actually managed to study all those works. Furthermore, some of the titles from the 1960s to the 1990s are no longer available. New readers would find it difficult to find "all of [my] books."

Evidence of the Gods is a collection in which those who have indeed read all of my books will find little that is new. Yet, this book is nevertheless different from the others. My archive contains more than 60,000 photos. I have assembled almost 200 of them in three chapters, in a way that will give rise to renewed wonder among both old and new readers. After all, who knows that in the huge expanse of the Pacific Ocean there are ruins and legends which belong together? Who has taken the trouble to examine the rock drawings and geoglyphs throughout the world for motifs relating to the gods? Who still remembers that there are stone structures in ancient Europe that do not fit anywhere into the Stone Age?

These riddles should be talked about to a greater extent. They exist. My pictures show it, and I have provided a thorough commentary. My aim is to present a new volume with exciting, previously unpublished pictures each year for the next several years.

Yours,

Erich von Däniken

July 2012

Chapter 1

ISLANDS
IN THE
PACIFIC

━━━━━━

Aside from where the tourists go, there are buildings whose origins are riddles and whose purpose is still not understood, such as those in the expanses of the blue Pacific. That is where Pohnpei is located, which is, at 540 km², the largest of the Caroline Islands. Various small islands surround Pohnpei, and one of them, a mere 0.44 km² in size, is called Temwen. This diminutive, tropical islet is a little bit smaller than Vatican City, yet it bears a monumental riddle: the ruins of Nan Madol.

These buildings consist of tens of thousands of hexagonal basalt columns stacked on top of one another, block house style, like heavyweight matches. Is there historical information about Pohnpei and its island satellites? (Image 1)

- In 1595, the first European man, the Portuguese Pedro Fernandes de Quiros, circumnavigated the island group in the *San Jeronimo* and dropped anchor off Nan Madol. The walls of Pohnpei appeared in the faint light like an other-worldly palace. Not a human soul anywhere.

- In 1826, the Irish seaman James O'Connell was shipwrecked off Pohnpei. He succeeded in reaching the safety of land with six other survivors. He married the 14-year-old daughter of the king of the island and remained there for 11 years, until a ship picked him up and took him back to Ireland.

- In 1851, the indigenous people massacred the crew of an English ship. In response, the British navy created a bloodbath on the island.

- From 1880 onward, Christian missionaries from various groups traveled to Temwen. Stone tablets with unfamiliar writing were destroyed in the ruins of Nan Madol; the ancient customs were forbidden.

- In 1886, the whole island group was annexed by Spain. The new owners called it the Caroline Islands, because Charles II was on the throne.

- In 1899, Spain sold the Carolines to the German Empire.

- In 1910, the native inhabitants rebelled. Missionaries and officials were murdered. Only a few Europeans escaped the massacre.

- In 1911, the German cruiser *Emden* shelled the islands. The rebels were slaughtered without mercy, their leaders hanged from palm trees.

- In 1919, Germany had lost the First World War, and Japan received a mandate to administer all the Caroline Islands.

- In 1944, during the Second World War, the American navy occupied the islands. Wealthy Japanese were expelled.

- In 1947, the islands were declared a trust territory of the United States.

What Was Nan Madol?

Anyone who visited the ruins of Nan Madol in their checkered history was faced with a riddle. How did the tens of thousands of basalt blocks arrive on the tiny island? What methods were used to lift the blocks, weighing up to 20 tonnes each? The highest wall still stands at 14.3 meters high, higher than a three-story building. (Images 2–5) What did the ground consist of? A substrate of coral will not bear heavy buildings of the dimensions of Nan Madol. Indeed, what was the purpose of the complex? What was there to defend on a tiny island very distant from any civilization in the South Pacific?

Basalt is cooled lava, and there is, indeed, a basalt quarry on the north coast of Pohnpei. It is about 25 kilometers distant from Nan Madol. Basalt can come out of the earth in various forms—in Pohnpei, it is in the form of polygonal columns. It is thought that the builders of Nan Madol suspended the basalt columns under their canoes or rafts to reduce their weight. Then they waited for high tide and rowed the heavy cargo to Nan Madol. Why were

2

3

4

EVIDENCE OF THE GODS

5

the buildings not erected directly on the "basalt island" of Pohnpei itself? What was so important about Nan Madol? Furthermore, Nan Madol consists of numerous canals, some of them as small as 2 meters in width. How were the basalt transporters supposed to have been maneuvered around the bends into the canals? This transport method relied on the alternation of high and low tide to work. The workers had to wait for low tide to attach the basalt columns under the rafts, then for high tide to transport them. How many rafts might have been in use at the same time in this endless exercise with low and high tides? How many ropes made of coconut fiber were required; how many trees were felled for the rafts?

Nan Madol is a mighty complex consisting of canals, ditches, tunnels, staircases, earthworks, and walls. (Images 6–13) The rectangular main district is stepped in terraces and surrounded by more than 80 smaller sub-districts. I took the trouble to count the basalt blocks on one side of a building. There were 1,082 columns.

The complex is square, which means that the four walls are made up of 4,328 columns. Then there is the floor, also made of basalt, the staircases, and terraces. In total, there are about 10,000 blocks for a single structure. An estimate for the total Nan Madol complex produces about 180,000 blocks—not including the substructure lying under water.

Nan Madol is not a "beautiful" city, although today it is described as "the Venice of the South Pacific." There are no reliefs, no sculptures, no statutes, and no paintings. The architecture is cold, forbidding, in some ways raw and threatening—not something we associate with a royal palace. Was the whole thing a defensive complex? Why, then, do broad staircases send out exactly the opposite message? Welcome! At the center of the complex, there is a "well," which isn't one. A well in this location, surrounded by salt water, does not make any sense at all, because it could only supply salt water. The native inhabitants describe the "well" as an entrance to the start or end of a tunnel. Today the opening lies almost 2 meters under water, even at low tide. Where is this tunnel supposed to have gone? How were the native peoples supposed to have built it under water? Everything in Nan Madol is a contradiction.

I read in Herbert Rittlinger's book, *Der maßlose Ozean*, that, thousands of years ago, Nan Madol formed the center of a glorious empire. The reports of fabulous treasure had attracted pearl fishers and Chinese traders to explore the ocean floor secretly. The divers had returned from the depths with incredible tales of "streets and stone arches, monoliths and the remains of houses."[1]

In 1908, a German expedition explored Pohnpei and Nan Madol. Dr. Paul Hambruch focused his work particularly on Nan Madol and the indigenous sagas and myths.[2] According to Hambruch, two young magicians once wanted to build a large cultural center for gods and spirits. They tried at various sites on the coast, but each time the wind and waves destroyed their work.

6

7

8

9

EVIDENCE OF THE GODS

Finally, they found the right place on Temwen. In response to a magic incantation, the basalt columns flew by themselves from the island of Jokaz to Temwen and put themselves in the right order without any human intervention. That was how Nan Madol was created. (Images 14–21)

Ancient Truths From the South Pacific

Originally, the German ethnologist Paul Hambruch writes in the second volume of his *Ergebnisse der Südsee-Expedition*,[3] a fire-breathing dragon had been the symbol of Nan Madol. The mother of the dragon had scooped out the canals with her mighty snorting. A magician had ridden on the dragon. When he spoke a particular incantation in verse form, the basalt columns from the neighboring island had flown there by themselves and had formed themselves into the walls.

Dragons? Fire-breathing? Magic incantations? Total nonsense at first sight. But how were Stone Age peoples supposed to have imagined a noisy monster, as excellently demonstrated in the science fiction film *Avatar*? A technical monster for which their language had no words? Incidentally, the dragon motif is a global element of many myths. The most ancient sagas of the Chinese refer to fire-breathing dragons, as do the Maya in Central America, the pre-Inca tribes in Bolivia, the Tibetans in their highlands, and even the Swiss in the Bernese Oberland. Excuse me?

I live in a small village, Beatenberg, a delightful place in the mountains above Lake Thun. There is a limestone cave below me in the rock: the dwelling of the former dragon. So an artificial dragon was put at the end of the cave, with dramatic lighting for the tourists. And the emblem of my village shows a picture of the dragon.[4] Other legends about Nan Madol say that the ruins were the remains of the fabled kingdom of Lemuria.[5]

10

11

EVIDENCE OF THE GODS

12

13

EVIDENCE OF THE GODS

14

Before the Second World War, Japanese divers are said to have discovered sarcophagi with platinum bars in the depths under Nan Madol. Tall tales? It has not, to date, been possible to solve the riddle of Pohnpei with the ruins of Nan Madol. And there is a connection with legends and structures on various islands in the South Pacific. ("South Pacific" is used here only as a collective term; it refers to the gigantic area of the Pacific south of the equator.)

As long ago as 1880, the ethnologist John White collected traditions from the South Pacific, which take on a completely new meaning when looked at from a modern perspective. Thus the Rongomai legend refers to a tribe called Ngati Haua, which sought protection against attack in a fortified village. Finally, they asked for help from their god Rongomai: "His appearance was like a shining star, like a fiery flame, like a sun."[6]

Rongomai descended to the village square: "The earth was churned up, clouds of dust obscured the view, the noise was like thunder, then like the murmur of a sea shell."[7]

Compare that with a legend from a completely different geographical area:

> ...strike down the enemy before you in the briefest time. Thereupon Hor-Hut flew up to the sun in the form of a sun disc with wings attached...when he saw the enemy from heavenly heights...he charged down upon them with such might that they neither saw with their eyes nor heard with their ears...Hor-Hut, shining in many different colors, returned to the ship Ra Harmachis in his shape as a large, winged sun disc.[8]

Is that allowed? To compare an ancient Egyptian account with a legend from the distant South Pacific? We have to! We no longer live in an age of isolation.

15

16

On the island of Raivavae in French Polynesia, the ancient temple of Te Mahara is still today deemed to be the point at which the mythological god Maui landed after his space flight.[9] The same applies to the original inhabitants of Atuona, a small island in the Marquesas group. There, mount Kei Ani is considered to be a temple, although there are no buildings at the site. The original Polynesians called the mountain Tautini Etua, literally, "mountain on which the gods landed."[10]

It is said about the creator god Ta'aroa of the Society Islands in the Pacific: "Ta'aroa sat in his sea shell, in the darkness for all eternity. The sea shell was like an egg which drifted in endless space. There was no heaven, no land, no sea, no moon, no sun, no stars. All was darkness."[11]

And on the Samoan islands this is reported about the original god Tagaloa: "God Tagaloa swam in the void; he created everything. Before him there was no heaven, no land, he was all alone and slept in the expanses of space. Neither was there any sea, nor was the earth at that time. His name was Tagaloa-fa'atutupu-nu'u, which means 'Origin of Growth.'"[12]

Does the Bible say anything different? Genesis 1:1–3 says, "In the beginning God created the heaven and the earth. And the earth was without form, and void; and darkness was upon the face of the deep. And the Spirit of God moved upon the face of the waters. And God said, Let there be light: and there was light..."[13] Later the Biblical god created plants, animals, and the human being. Growth only came after the landing. No different from Tagaloa-fa'atutupu-nu'u.

The originator of Melanesian culture, Suganainoni by name, is said to have descended from heaven in "smoke and fire"[14] and to have disappeared again in an equally spectacular fashion. At the time, giants are said to have tried to build a giant stairway to heaven, an endeavor that was thwarted by the god Suganainoni. Is this a parallel to the Tower of Babel?

17

The South Pacific Islands are full of similar legends, and it is always possible to find a connection with the traditions in other parts of the world. Such a job was actually undertaken several decades ago. In an extensive tome, the ethnologist Karl Kohlenberg published hundreds of mythological links spanning the world.[15] No discipline in ethnology has ever shown any interest in this. Ethnology appears to have become stuck in the century before last.

Thirty years ago, I spent some weeks on Kiribati, a group of 16 islands which, until 1977, were part of the British crown colony of the Gilbert Islands. Then the islands became independent and changed their name. Even today, the native inhabitants mostly live in simple straw huts with roofs made of palm leaves. (Image 22) At only about 973 km², the Kiribati islands ride the Pacific and provide solid ground underfoot for about 60,000 Micronesians. According to the latest research, Kiribati has been inhabited for

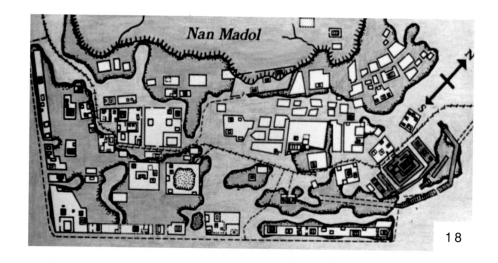

Nan Madol

18

at least 3,000 years. Three thousand years without written records is a long time. In Tarawa, the main city of the islands, I immersed myself in the legends. They were not collected and published until the last century by indigenous researchers. And once again, it all started in space.[16]

The Story of Nareau

A long, long time ago, there was the god Nareau. No one knows from whence he came or who his parents were, *because Nareau flew alone and sleeping through space.* In sleep he heard his name being called three times, but the caller was "nobody." Nareau woke up and looked around. There was nothing but emptiness, but when he looked down, he saw a large object. It was Te Bomatemaki, meaning "Earth and sky together." Nareau's curiosity led him to descend and carefully set foot on Te Bomatemaki. There were no living beings there, no animals, no humans. Just him, the creator. Four times he circumnavigated the world he had found from north to south, east to west, and he was alone. Finally Nareau dug a hole in Te Bomatemaki, filled it with water and sand, mixed both into rock, and ordered the rock and the void to give birth to Nareau Tekikiteia. Thereupon Nareau created the plants, animals, and human beings, whom he taught language. Then he decided to separate heaven from earth.

The ethnologist Arthur Grimble provided an important addition: "And when the work was done, Nareau, the creator, said: 'Enough! It has been done! I go, never to return!' So he went, never to return, and no one knows where he has been since then."[17]

The first beings endowed with reason had to memorize words, which give us food for thought:

- *Nabawe* meaning "the essence of age."
- *Karitoro* meaning "the essence of energy."
- *Kanaweawe* meaning "the essence of dimension."
- *Ngkoangkoa* meaning "the essence of time."
- *Auriaria* meaning "the essence of light."
- *Nei Tewenei* meaning "comet" or "movement in the sky."

I keep hearing arrogant critics who don't know anything—or at best might have studied a few semesters of ethnology, and then only in relation to a restricted geographical area—say that common features are of no significance. They can be explained psychologically. Here Carl Gustav Jung (1875–1961) is always cited to lend support. He saw the myths of ancient civilizations as "archetypical developments of consciousness" in which the "collective unconscious" found its correspondence of good and evil, joy and punishment, life and death. For his theories of "individuation" and the "archetype," Jung has to fall back on innate behaviors. Human beings had always wanted to be like birds. So the legends about flying had arisen.

What age are we living in? These psychological explanations not only stick in my craw, they are also totally divorced from reality. They attempt to destroy the common narrative of ancient peoples with the drip of psychological acid. All that remains is meaningless smugness.

19

20

EVIDENCE OF THE GODS

On the basis of the knowledge we have today, the pattern associated with the creator Nareau (and others!) makes sense. Imagine a spaceship in which the pilot (presumably with the whole crew) lies in deep sleep. This option of deep sleep to keep astronauts alive over long distances has long been the subject of discussion in space medicine. At some point, the ship's sensors determine that a solar system has been reached and the on-board computer wakes the pilot. *Nareau flew alone and sleeping through space, in sleep he heard his name being called three times, but the caller was nobody.*

The commander, who has now awoken back to life, still sees the blackness of space around him but below him also a planet. *Nareau awoke and looked around him. There was nothing but emptiness, but when he looked down he saw a large object. It was Te Bomatemaki, meaning "Earth and sky together."*

Nareau risks a landing, and examines the ground and the composition of the air. He determines the absence of any life. *Nareau's curiosity led him to descend and carefully set foot on Te Bomatemaki. There were no living beings there, no animals, no humans. Just him, the creator.* The initial exploration is insufficient. What do the other continents look like? So he circumnavigates the whole planet several times to assure himself that he has not invaded foreign sovereign territory. *Four times he circumnavigated the world he had found from north to south, east to west, and he was alone.*

With the technology he had available, Nareau quickly found ways to water the earth. Plant seeds, of which there were plenty on board, were taken down, and finally living beings were created. A genetic seed bank is required to create life forms. That, precisely, is likely to be part of the standard inventory on an interstellar space ship. The space travelers are unlikely to be able to tell from their distant home planet which planets provide the conditions for life, but do not have life on them. But why create life at all? The space travelers must survive, replenish their food stocks. That requires food and drink—organic material.

21

The Biblical creation story reports exactly the same thing. In it, God collects water and creates grasses, herbs, and trees. (Genesis 1: 9–12) Only then did the animals in the water, air, and on land follow—each one after their kind. And as the crowning event, he creates the human being—in his own image.

Astonishingly, the creation story of Nareau includes concepts such as "essence of energy," "essence of dimension," "essence of time," and "essence of light." Under "essence of light," we might imagine a photon drive which can propel a spaceship to incredible speeds. But each acceleration is tied to the "essence of dimension." Bridging huge distances is, in turn, linked to the "essence of time" and the age— the survival—of the crew (the "essence of age"). Makes a lot of sense, actually. For millennia, we were simply unable to understand it. Looked at from the perspective of the dawning space age, the veils are lifting.

Taboo Points and Navigation Stones

Even today the inhabitants of Kiribati fear certain locations on the islands which are deemed to be "taboo points," because "mighty spirits" were once at work there. With the assistance of the inhabitants, I was once allowed to visit two such taboo points on the southern tip of the island of Arorae. (Arorae belongs to Kiribati. Not to be confused with the island of Aurora.) There was a square hemmed in with stones on the ground. (Image 23) That was supposed to be a taboo point? As I tried to step into the rectangle, my companions held me back: "No! Please don't step in there!" When I enquired further as to why not, I was told that anyone who walked over the square fell ill. The birds did not fly over it either. Indeed, not even weeds were growing inside the square. I obeyed the warning.

The second taboo point turned out to be a low, rectangular wall. An opening had been left in the middle like a well. (Image 24) I looked inside, but there was no water. The native inhabitants declared that if I held my hand over it, the hairs on the back of my hand would rise. I tried it and did indeed feel something like a pulsation.

The island of Arorae is just 4 kilometers long and a few hundred meters wide. At its southern tip, weather-worn rectangular stone blocks rise from the ground. Each block has a groove on its top edge, and each stone points in a different direction. My companions enlightened me that these were "navigation stones." (Images 25 and 26)

What on earth were they? Two or more were made of granite, which is not found on the island; the others showed characteristics of basalt. Each stone, I learned, pointed to a different island. The ancestors had taken a bearing on distant destinations using the navigation stones before paddling off in their decorated canoes.

In my black bag, which has accompanied me for decades, there is also a map of the Pacific region and a compass. I aligned the map and compass and stood behind the stones. One groove indicating

22

23

EVIDENCE OF THE GODS

24

25

south pointed without deviation toward the island of Niutao, 1,800 kilometers away (linear distance). Niutao is part of the Ellice Islands. A longer line pointed precisely to West Samoa, a distance of 1,900 kilometers away (linear distance) to the east of the Fiji Islands. With a third line I took a bearing on the 4,700 kilometer-distant (linear distance) Tuamotu Islands in the southern Pacific. How could that be? Did the inhabitants of Kiribati know about the compass?

As one of my companions assured me with visible pride, yes! The ancestors had received the compass and instructions on how to use it from a god. He had been so large and strong that he could pick coconuts from the crowns of palm trees and also crush them in his hand. He had also "imprinted" his footsteps in the soil as a reminder.[18] They had venerated these footprints long before the Christian missionaries arrived. I photographed them. (Image 27)

26

27

Evidence in stone honoring the gods exists throughout the scattered islands of the South Pacific. These structures, which are not understood, are mostly called *marae* and the reason for their existence is disputed. There is such a marae, a holy site, even on the world-famous tourist island of Tahiti. (Image 28) On the island of Raiatea in French Polynesia, there is a monolith in the center of the marae, which is said to be ensouled by *mana*. (Images 29–32) Mana is here considered to be a pulsation that can heal disease.

A terrible yet instructive legend throughout the South Pacific region, which is ascribed to the Maoris in New Zealand, is the story of the bird Rupe. Hina, a sister of the divine bird Rupe, is said once to have been made pregnant by a human being. He hid Hina on a distant island, in a house which was surrounded by a "protective screen." This protective screen prevented any access from outside and made it impossible for Hina to leave her prison. As the hour when she was due to give birth neared, no one was able to assist her. In her suffering, she called out "Rupe! Rupe! Please help me!"[19] Soon

28

there was a loud noise over the house, and the divine Rupe called to his sister, "Hina, I am here."

But Rupe was only able to reach his sister after he had broken through the "protective screen." After giving birth, Hina asked her brother to fly her back home. But first he was to evacuate the inhabitants of the island. Rupe said that in order to do so he would have to make the flight three times, because there was not enough space on his back. So the islanders seated themselves on Rupe, who flew them far out over the ocean where he tipped them into the water. Finally, he collected Hina and her infant. Flying high up, Hina saw pieces of clothing that had belonged to the islanders floating on the ocean waves and asked her brother Rupe why he had killed the people. He answered, "They wronged you while you were living on their island. They locked you up and no one helped you at the birth. That is why I grew angry and threw them all into the ocean." A brutal way to teach people to be helpful!

29

30

EVIDENCE OF THE GODS

31

32

33

34

Yesterday's Opinions

In the mass of literature on ethnology, I keep stumbling upon preconceived doctrines which were set down in these books in the last century or earlier, and which no one dares to challenge. Eyes have become blind, thoughts dull. Science, I read, cannot accept fantastical solutions, because they have no empirical foundation that can be verified. In fact, there are most certainly artifacts which can be verified by looking at them and which support the myths. Outdated views, no doubt espoused 60 years ago by learned scholars, are in my eyes growing more fantastical and incredible by the day, while a contemporary way of looking at things is gaining a solid foundation. Three prerequisites form the basis of all research: freedom of thought, the gift of observation, and a sense of context. I would like to add a fourth one to that: overcoming the spirit of the times.

35

It is not just in Indonesia that the multi-purpose bird Garuda—the mount of the god Vishnu—haunts the immortal traditions. (Image 33) Garuda independently dropped bombs, extinguished conflagrations, flew to the moon, and also transported people—as required. His depictions and reliefs in innumerable temples belong to the empirically verifiable foundation of Garuda research. Why should the same principle not apply to the gods of the South Pacific such as Rupe, Nareau, Tagaloa, Rongomai, or Pourangahua? The latter is part of the Maori legends of New Zealand and belongs as much to the flyers of antiquity as Garuda.

36

37

42 EVIDENCE OF THE GODS

38

39

EVIDENCE OF THE GODS

40

The god Pourangahua flew on a "magic bird" from Hawaiki to New Zealand. Tradition tells about this god Pourangahua: "I come and an unknown earth lies beneath my feet. I come and a new sky revolves above me. I come and the earth is a peaceful resting place for me."[20] The empirical foundation is provided by comparative mythology and the depictions of these gods in wood and stone.

Ceremonial Stuff and Ritual Masks

Every year, rituals in honor of the ancient goods take place on the Fiji Islands. The masks worn by the dancers are bird masks (Image 34)—not, as psychologists would have you believe, because people have always had the desire to be like birds, but simply because the people of the South Pacific imitated their ancient gods. And in their world of ideas, they could fly. Thus in the often small museums in the Pacific region, we find so-called ritual clothing, ritual masks, ceremonial masks, or ritual props, which refer to ancient one-man flying machines. Image 35 shows the upper part of the Indonesian (also Indian) god Garuda. Here the two vertical pieces of wood symbolize the wings. The same motif can be seen in several manifestations in the Bishop Museum in Honolulu, Hawaii. Images 36 and 37 show such ritual masks, which the dancers pull on over their heads. The upper arms are passed through the semi-circles at the bottom, depicting the flapping of wings when they are moved up and down. Image 38 shows such a wing mask in the rest position. The arm and other supports, often the whole corset itself into which the dancers had to squeeze themselves, have been remembered in the folklore for thousands of years. Images 39 and 40 illustrate the seated position of the ancient flyers as imagined by the artists. Image 41 shows a rather technical-looking flying fish carrying three people. The posture of the central figure appears to indicate that this is the "pilot." A comparison of the image of the god Maui on the "fish" and the (alleged) ruler Pacal on the lid of the tomb in Palenque in Mexico (Image 42) speaks volumes. The two pictures should be looked at both horizontally and vertically. As the Biblical prophet Ezekial said, "They have eyes to see and see not."

The capital of Tonga, the island group of south-western Polynesia, is called Nukualofa. There, on the main island of Tongatabu, tourists can admire various temple terraces, several stories high, which are still considered to be holy sites today. The largest monolithic structure is called Ha'amonga (Images 43 and 44), a stone gateway through which the god Rongomai will ceremoniously step at some time in the future. His return is anticipated like that of all the other gods.

Easter Island belongs into the extensive South Pacific chapter as much as Kiribati or Temwen. But so much has already been written about Easter Island—including by me!—that I only want to touch on the subject briefly. In doing so, I will add to the list of questions that are still unanswered despite all the research and literature.

41

42

43

Questions About Easter Island

Whom did the Easter Islanders actually want to depict with their statues? Some chief? The deceased race of highly venerated ancestors? Foreign visitors? The statues are most certainly not images of themselves. The inhabitants of the island are people with soft features, the slightly thick lips and broad noses of all Polynesians. The eyes are almond-shaped, the chin softly rounded.

44

The Easter Island statues, by contrast, depict robot-like, dull faces with small lips tightly pressed together, long, pointed noses, and deep-set eyes. They do not fit in with any cultural image. *Whom*, then, did the Easter Islanders chisel into stone? *Whom* did they venerate or fear? Which force—or belief, if you like—spurred them on to such labor?

45

EVIDENCE OF THE GODS

46

The statues are said to have been created "only recently"—about 800 to, at most, 1,500 years ago. Such dating is based on charcoal remains and bones. The only problem is that these dates do not in any way explain the meter-thick layer of rubble which covered the statues. (Image 45) When they were discovered, only the heads were sticking out of the ground. The actual body was buried in the earth. I am lucky enough to have photographed Easter Island 50 years ago, at a time when it was not yet a tourist destination. The pictures document it. Of course, I am aware that Thor Heyerdahl[21] found hundreds of fist-sized rocks beside the unfinished statues. It was concluded from this that they had been used to hew the figures out of the rock. But the distances between the rock and statues are up to 1.84 meters. (Image 46)

And one of the statues in the Rano Raraku crater is 31.4 meters long. That cannot be done with fist-sized rocks. Do the thrown-away rocks simply prove that the work could not be done with them? The work was not finished, after all; the unfinished statues show that.

The indigenous inhabitants describe their tiny island as the "navel of the world."[22] Such a name can only be given if there is an awareness of at least a few other countries. Within a radius of 1,500 kilometers, there is merely one other tiny island. Then there is nothing else for a long, long time.

A public festival is still held today in which brave young men have to find an egg on a small rocky reef off the island and bring it back undamaged to the main island. Originally, it is said to have symbolized the egg of a birdman. Several stone eggs have been found among the rocks on Easter Island. (Images 47 and 48) They have an impressive diameter of up to 1 meter.

Birdman? South Pacific legends? There are rock engravings on Easter Island which show a hybrid creature consisting of a human being and bird in a squatting position. (Image 49) There are other misunderstood rock carvings on small walls, cave walls, or large slabs of rock, which wait unnoticed by the coast to be deciphered. (Images 50–53)

The figures originally wore red hats with a respectable head size. (Images 54–56) Were these hats intended to indicate the same thing as the "helmets" or "haloes" which can be found in rock art throughout the world?

There still remains the riddle of the writing. At one time, some of the statues wore small wooden tablets around their neck. Two of them are exhibited in the anthropological museum of Santiago de Chile. The engravings show a certain affinity with the writing of Mohenjo-daro, an ancient Indus Valley civilization (modern-day Pakistan). Only the dating does not fit. The settlement of Easter Island is thought to have occurred about 350 AD; the Mohenjo-daro civilization existed more than 2,000 years earlier. Nothing adds up.

47

48

49

EVIDENCE OF THE GODS

50

51

52

53

EVIDENCE OF THE GODS

54

The latest theory about Easter Island comes from the German archeologist Kurt Horedt.[23] He discovered a remarkable similarity between Germanic runes and the illegible characters of Easter Island. Two lines of inscription with nine runes were discovered near Gallehus in Northern Schleswig (Germany) in the 16th and 17th century. Seven of them reappear in almost identical form on the wooden tablets of Easter Island. How is that possible?

Did northern Germanic peoples end up on Easter Island 1,500 years ago? That would also explain the features of the statues on Easter Island, according to the archeologist Kurt Horedt. Even the

55

56

EVIDENCE OF THE GODS

red hats on the heads of the statues could be identical with the shock of red hair of the Teutons. Was it ancient Germanic peoples, then, who served as a model for the statues? Shipwrecked sailors, perhaps, who set up all the statues around the shore of the island to draw attention to themselves? Were they supposed to draw the attention of the crews of other Germanic vessels who happened to have strayed into the area? After all, radio did not exist at the time.

Nothing is impossible. The thing that puzzles me is merely the question: how did Germanic peoples—long before Columbus!—get from the North Atlantic to the South Pacific?

Boulders on the Beach

North of Dunedin in New Zealand, there are about 100 spherical boulders lying on Moeraki Beach. The largest has a diameter of 3.16 meters. These giant geodes are literally flushed out of the rock, roll a few meters, come to a halt, and are then washed over by the daily tides. (Images 57 and 58) Many have broken apart, crumbling away as the result of the action of wind and waves. No one has any idea how many of the boulders have already been swallowed by the surf, worn down over thousands of years. (Images 59 and 60) Yet the rock keeps flushing out new boulders from the sediment as if a rock mother were laying eggs.

Geologists assure us that this is a perfectly natural process. The boulders are formed through the deposit of calcite in soft sandstone. This calcite forms a core around which the rock solidifies over millennia, rather like a pearl around a grain of sand. The comparison is flawed, however, because the oyster with the pearl is constantly in motion in the water; the rock, by contrast, does not move. Why, actually, does this geological miracle not happen on many other beaches around the world? And why would rock solidify around the calcite core *as a ball*? (Images 60–63)

57

58

EVIDENCE OF THE GODS

59

60

61

62

EVIDENCE OF THE GODS

63

The Maoris, the original inhabitants of New Zealand, call these boulders Te Kai-hinaki. The composite word consists of *kai*, meaning "food," and *hinai*, meaning "basket." An infinitely long time ago, the ship Arai-te-uru had been destroyed while searching for valuable gems. A hill not far from the beach showed the petrified hull of the vessel. The boulders that keep emerging from the rock contain the food (energy?), which fell out of the baskets when the ship was destroyed. Strange story.

Impossible, Yet Real

Even stranger is the story of a spherical rock that was found on February 13, 1961, 6 miles north-east of Olancha at the edge of the Amargosa desert in California. At the time, Mike Mikesell, Wallace Lane, and Virginia Maxey were looking for minerals and were particularly on the lookout for geodes. The three owned a souvenir shop in Olancha, and they knew very well that geodes could be sold for a lot of money. This is because there are magnificent crystals inside a geode. About 120 meters above Owens Lake, the three discovered an irregularly shaped geode and laboriously hauled their find home. The next day, Mike Mikesell wanted to saw the rock in half to get to the crystals on the inside. As always, he used a diamond saw. Suddenly the saw snapped. A new saw blade suffered the same fate. Now the hard-working finders suspected that there might be a particularly valuable mineral inside the geode, perhaps even a diamond. They finally succeeded in splitting the geode in half with a great deal of effort and the assistance of a hammer and chisel. Their surprise could not have been greater: The outer skin consisted of a layer of sea fossils. This was followed by a layer that reminded them of petrified wood. Finally, there were two rings of a porcelain-like material, which in turn contained a plain pin 2 millimeters in diameter and 17 millimeters in length. (Images 64 and 65) That is what had broken the diamond saw. Geologists, none of whom want to reveal their name, estimate the age of the geode at about 500,000 years.

What is it that does not fit about the earth's past? It is completely impossible that the plain pin, whose composition has never been discovered, could have entered the geode from the outside. After all, the pin assumes a high level of knowledge of metallurgy of some kind—and of a workshop—500,000 years ago.

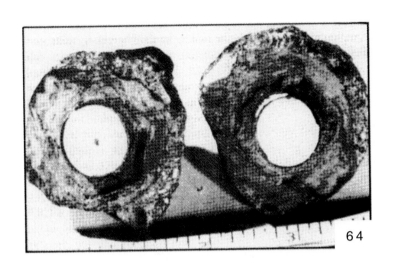

64

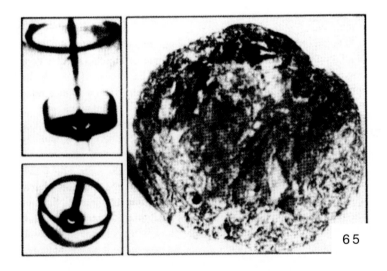

65

66 EVIDENCE OF THE GODS

Chapter 2

SALUTING

THE

GODS

———

There was a time, and it lies in the far distant past, when our ancestors had not yet mastered writing. How were messages to be left for future generations? Where could people draw and paint—for their own pleasure—and proudly show the results of such new art to the members of their tribe? The people of the Stone Age across the world all had the same idea. They decided to chisel drawings and engravings into the rock and cave walls.

From a present perspective, that represents an incredible research field. At first, this field may seem, perhaps, just as boring as collecting stamps...until the collector suddenly sees the light. There is something fascinating about this millennia-old art form, celebrated by peoples who knew nothing about one another and were incapable of knowing anything about one another. Why? What is so interesting about boring rock drawings? They exist in Yemen, in the Mato Grosso rainforest of Brazil, and on the coast of southern Chile. From Hawaii to central China, from Siberia to South Africa, we find these pictorial greetings from the people of the Stone Age, postcards from a far-distant past. In very few

67

68

EVIDENCE OF THE GODS

instances do we know the tribes which scribbled on their rocks, and thus many a Stone Age people posthumously obtained their name—christened by contemporary science.

How many rock drawings might there be worldwide? There must be millions of them. Even small islands and the highest mountains can yield petroglyphs—the technical term for these rock engravings. They exist in Ice-Age Alaska as much as on the blisteringly hot rock walls of the Kimberley range in Australia, in California, on Easter Island, or in the Indus Valley in Pakistan. And the incredible thing about them is the motifs.

Now, it is not surprising that Stone Age people kept depicting hunting scenes. The sun, moon, circles, matchstick figures, and handprints are also part of everyday life. I could show several thousand examples of this kind of rock drawing. My archive is full of them. There are many photographic volumes with such pictures; I only refer to the most important ones in the References (Numbers 1–11 under "Saluting the Gods"). What is the difference between other photographic books with rock drawings and this one? Other researchers always concentrated on one specific geographic area. But it only becomes interesting once specific forms are given the same attributes everywhere, as if talking drums had carried the message across all continents: the gods are the ones with the rays! My purpose is the intercontinental comparison of these amazing figures.

Connections Between Continents?

Australia lies a long way from the other continents, and in prehistoric times, the original inhabitants of Australia, the Aborigines, doubtlessly had no contact with the rest of the world. Yet, whole picture galleries by the indigenous inhabitants were created, primarily in the Kimberley range in the northwest of the continent. The motifs keep repeating themselves: gods with gleaming faces,

69

70

EVIDENCE OF THE GODS

with radiating auras around their heads—indeed, with suits enclosing their bodies. In 1981, I took hundreds of photographs, some of them in magnificent color, and kept asking myself the same question: what did the indigenous inhabitants use as a model? There is an elongated figure with two "antennae." (Image 66) Then there are gods and goddesses with large eyes and goggles. The Aborigines call them *wondinas*, mother goddesses. One large figure is lying horizontally (Image 67); she seems to be wearing some kind of coat. The angel-like head in Image 68 has lines on both sides, as if they were messages. Although the wondina figures all appear in the same colors and with the same faces, they are nevertheless different depictions. Take a look at the accompanying drawings in Images 69 and 70. At a brief glance, one might think the figure with the outstretched arms and legs (Images 71 and 72) is the same. Not so. The "garland" around the radiant head, the different widths of the tongue, and the boomerang-like object at the bottom right prove it. It is missing in the one picture. The two beings with rays around their heads in Images 73 and 74 are not identical either. The large figure on Image 75 has a second, much larger radiating aura over its "halo." The subject of special veneration? When the German flyer Hans Bertram had to make an emergency landing in the Kimberley mountains in October 1940, he was only spared by the Aborigines because he was wearing flying goggles with a wide leather rim. The indigenous inhabitants saw him as a messenger of wondina.

There are several thousand of these rock drawings in Australia, made thousands of years ago by the original inhabitants, the Aborigines. In more recent times, some of them have been traced with colored chalk to make them more visible. Image 76 was left in its original state and a "round head" appears in Image 77, which could equally well be found on a rock wall in the Tassili N'Ajjer mountains in the Sahara. And that makes it inexplicable.

72

73

74 EVIDENCE OF THE GODS

75

76

Half the globe lies between the Algerian Sahara and the Kimberley mountains in Australia. Yet in the Tassili N'Ajjer massif in the Sahara, petroglyphs were discovered among hundreds of others that actually require no introduction. The first thing we recognize is the plump heads, then the puffed up suits. Because these rock drawings are very difficult to photograph, we sprinkled them with water to make the contours visible.

What stared back at us from the rock face here is described by archeologists as the "round head period." The largest figure measures 8 meters in height. Its discoverer, the French specialist in prehistory Henri Lhote, described it spontaneously as "the great Martian god."[11]

What was going on inside these Stone Age people, dressed in furs or naked, that they wanted to show something like this to posterity? What impressed them so hugely that they made the

77

78

79

EVIDENCE OF THE GODS

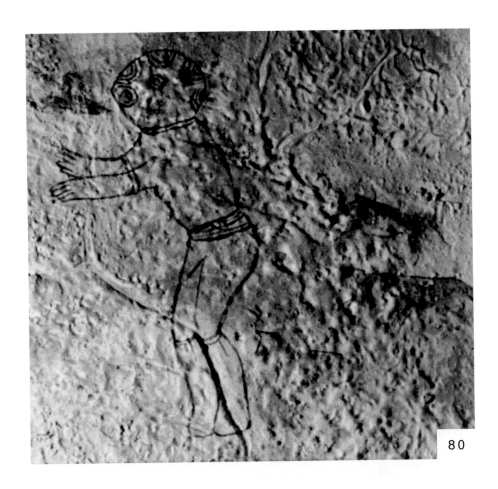

80

figure 8 meters high, towering over everything else? What did they see, what did they worship? The answer is staring us in the face. Images 78 and 79 are not the same. That can easily be seen in the helmet-like head. In Image 79, there are clear rings around the upper arms of this well-padded being, reinforcement rings not dissimilar to the ones in space suits. No psychological explanation can help us out here. Something mighty impressed the rock artists a great deal.

In Image 80, we traced the contours without adding a single extra line. What is unclear about that?

EVIDENCE OF THE GODS

81

82

Rock Drawings of the Hopi

We know the Native American Hopi rock drawings were both markings for fellow tribes and history books for their own people. The first world, Hopi tradition teaches, was Toktela. Literally Toktela means "infinite space."[12] This first world had been inhabited by only Taiowa, the creator. The ancestors had made contact with various worlds until they found their home on this planet. The supreme law was *you shall not kill any brother.* If over the course of time differences occurred between Hopi, the opposing parties separated and went off in separate directions in search of new hunting grounds. But each party kept to the ancient laws and, on its long marches, marked the rocks with inscriptions that could be read by their fellow tribesmen and women. Thus, these rock drawings are nothing other than messages to other Hopi who might pass at some later time. (Incidentally, the same thing was practiced by the ancestors of the Mormons.) Such messages might be, for example, "We have dug a well.... Deadly scorpions live here.... We have seen the gods." These drawings had the same value for the Native Americans of the time as the wall newspapers in China today. In 1982, when I was taking photographs at a Hopi rock massif not far from the hidden Hopi settlement of Oraibi in Arizona (Image 81), a Native American on a horse suddenly appeared and told me in no uncertain terms to stop. He even demanded that I hand over the films. Thankfully, White Bear, one of the Hopi elders, was with me and calmed down his young fellow tribesman. I was—White Bear said—one of the initiates.

The rocks are full of engravings—there must be thousands of them. (Images 82–85) Often they are positioned at a height of several meters. The artists must have built scaffolding or descended the walls on ropes. The highlighted Image 86 is called "The Starblower" by the Hopi.

EVIDENCE OF THE GODS

83

84

Images 87 and 88 both show the same motif, one of them highlighted. Beings from other worlds? The suspicion is confirmed in Images 89 and 90. An extraterrestrial and a UFO shape? And of course, in Hopi art, we also find art figures with rays and antenna-like structures on their heads, as well as *kachinas*, which have been immortalized in stone. (Image 91) According to Hopi tradition, the kachinas were the heavenly teachers of their ancestors.[13]

Today, kachinas are made in the form of wooden dolls and sold to tourists. The aim is to remind people of the former teachers, who promised to return one day. I have shown pictures of kachina dolls several times in previous books. Why again? Please compare the kachina dolls with the rock drawings. (Images 92–95) Something that was laboriously entrusted to the rock thousands of years ago is presented today much more simply in wooden form. The ancient

85

86

87

EVIDENCE OF THE GODS

88

89

90

92

motif remains the same. Kachinas were the teachers from the stars, and they were represented in a uniformly similar way around the globe—even in Val Camonica above the small town of Capo di Ponte in South Tyrol, Italy. There the rock drawings may be small compared to those in the Sahara or Australia, yet they fit just as much into the worldwide merry-go-round of the gods. Image 96 shows two figures with "haloes," just like at the bottom in Image 97. Archeologists interpret the figure as a "dancer." In Image 98, the "star with the planets" in the upper left corner of the picture stands out. Identical depictions can be admired on Sumerian cylinder seals.

Which psychology will provide yet another excuse for this phenomenon? The motifs of intercontinental rock art can of course be photographed. Our "Stone Agers" did not engage in global tourism. So only a single answer remains: they must have observed similar things. Something mighty and incomprehensible revealed itself worldwide, which imprinted itself on the minds of the Stone Age artists. And they left traces for eternity.

94

95

96

97

EVIDENCE OF THE GODS

98

Painters' Convention in Brazil?

In the vastness of Brazil, prehistoric finds are often the discovery of amateurs. The Austrian Ludwig von Schwennhagen was an amateur with an obsession. He lived as a philosophy and history teacher in Teresina, the capital of the northern Brazilian state of Piaui. He discovered a giant area with rock drawings, divided the region into seven districts, and called them Sete Cidades, or seven cities. His book about Sete Cidades[14] appeared in 1928, but it generated no great interest. Ludwig von Schwennhagen died as an impoverished school teacher.

Sete Cidades lies to the north of Teresina, between the towns of Piripiri and Rio Longe (about 3,000 kilometers north of Rio de Janeiro). The landscape is flat and of an intensive green, the roadsides lined with bushes. It alternates with sections of rainforest. Wild pigs, wild cows, and even wild horses make driving hazardous. Though Sete Cidades is almost at the equator, the climate is nevertheless bearable, because a light breeze is constantly blowing from the Atlantic coast 300 kilometers away. Sete Cidades is reached from Piripiri by a 16-kilometer-long road.

EVIDENCE OF THE GODS

EVIDENCE OF THE GODS

100

101

The visitor unexpectedly comes up against the rock walls. It is as if one were standing amidst burning chaos, torn apart like the Biblical Gomorrah, destroyed by fire and brimstone. A hill lies hidden beneath the shell of a tortoise—that, at least, is what it looks like, but science assures us that these are unusual forms of glacial deposits. (Image 99) Glacial deposits? Here? By the equator? When is that supposed to have happened? My escort, an official from the state of Piaui, offered another explanation: In earlier times, Sete Cidades had been an ocean basin and the strange rocks were nothing more than eroded rocks. Wind and weather had sculpted the curious forms over millennia. (Images 100 and 101)

EVIDENCE OF THE GODS

102

103

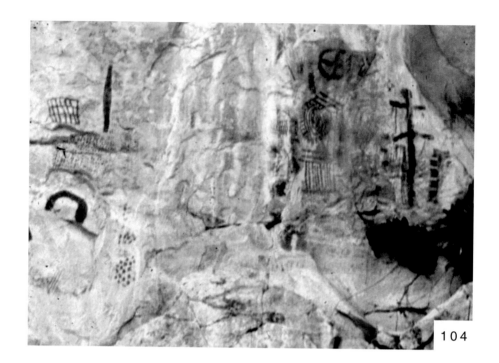

104

Even if the origin of the strange landscape formations remains a mystery, the rock drawings are a fact. There are tens of thousands of them. They cling to overhanging rocks (Image 102) or salute us from walls at a height of 15 meters (Image 103). Once again, the same questions arise as in the rock cauldron of the Hopi near Oraibi, Arizona: Did the artists build scaffolding? Descend on ropes? Pile stones on top of one another? Why so many colored drawings in a single place at all? A Stone Age meeting point? And, as if by agreement, those "gods" on the rock walls with their haloes, rays, or helmet-like forms around their heads. (Image 104)

Once again, even the cleverest mind under the sun does not know who painted or engraved the paintings on to the walls. Yet it quickly becomes clear that the prehistoric artists preferred the same motifs as their colleagues on the other side of the world: circles,

105

106

wheels with spokes, suns, squares, hand prints, crosses, stars, and highlighted beings. Additionally there are a few paintings that do not occur anywhere else. (Images 105–109) There are red and yellow circles, which today would be assigned signal character, bright red rings arranged above one another, or a round structure with a root-like outgrowth. In the round object, there is something like a small window. A UFO? Heaven help us! I cannot think of any reasonable explanations, the exception being my adored "gods." They greet us from the walls also in Sete Cidades, like everywhere. (Image 110) And all we can come up with for such a worldwide concurrence is a psychological angle? Our Stone Age ancestors are hardly likely to have all visited the same painting school. So where does the initial spark for these depictions of the gods come from? The gods are the ones with the rays!

107

108

EVIDENCE OF THE GODS

109

110

111

EVIDENCE OF THE GODS

112

You might think that Sete Cidades, with its impossible motifs on the rock walls, was probably a singular aberration of the Stone Age artists. What do we know about the Stone Age anyway? Maybe there was some kind of painters' convention every few years near the equator in Sete Cidades, and a few whiz-kids managed to get from California to Sete Cidades and back. Or perhaps they sent their latest creations around the world on some kind of hocus-pocus telepathic wave. I know that such a suggestion is ridiculous. That is why the question bothers me all the more as to why various rock paintings southeast of Santa Barbara, California, are similar to those in Sete Cidades. The art gallery of Santa Barbara is just as incomprehensible for us thinkers of the 21st century as the one in Sete Cidades. What else can one say except that in Santa Barbara, too, the large figures with the rays indicate the gods, no matter whether they are called "Great Manitou" or "Rongomai." Images 111–117 speak for themselves.

113

EVIDENCE OF THE GODS

114

115

116

117

EVIDENCE OF THE GODS

The people thousands of years ago left their god-like messages not just in rock drawings but also on the ground and on mountain slopes. The best-known example of this is the Nazca plains in Peru. I have written a separate book about the runway-like lines in the desert sand.[15] I will therefore refrain from discussing the kilometer-long lines. Here I will present a comparative study of similar motifs worldwide. The unsolved riddle lies in the little word "worldwide." It simply does not fit into the Stone Age.

Saluting the Gods

Alongside Las Pistas, as the indigenous people of Nazca call their lines, the area in and around Nazca is teeming with figures of gods with the same attributes as in the rock art. On the brow of a brown and rocky slope, my lens alighted on a "manikin" with large eyes and two antennae. (Image 118) There was a similar figure slightly lower on another hill. Here are the precise coordinates for photographers: latitude 14°42'26"S, longitude 75°6'38"W. The "antenna beings" cannot be overlooked. One figure is wearing a hat-like form with a wide brim and feelers sticking out of the headdress. The arms are spread wide in a dance-like gesture and the figure is grasping something with both hands which is not clearly defined. (Image 119) The object reminds me of similar things in the hands of the "dancers" of Val Camonica in South Tyrol. (Compare Images 96 and 112. Other ray beings are stuck on various mountain walls around Nazca, Image 120) They make more of an impression than any rock drawing and include some with an "antenna head" and rectangular body. (Image 121)

Then there are two very curious drawings next to one another. To the left in Image 122, the figure is wearing a flower-like decoration on its head. The whorl-covered body turns into strips with indecipherable symbols. A robot figure is right next to it (Image 123) from whose head straight "antennae" extend in every direction. The lower body widens like a skirt or wing. This depiction occupies a special place in my collection, because there is a copy of it in Chile.

118

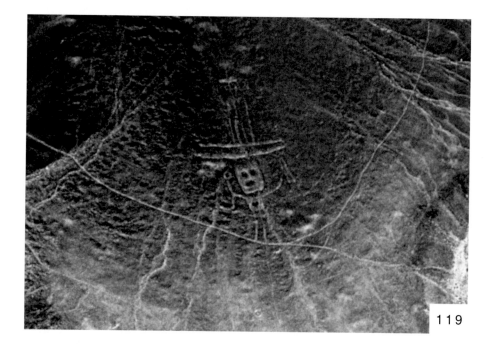

119

EVIDENCE OF THE GODS

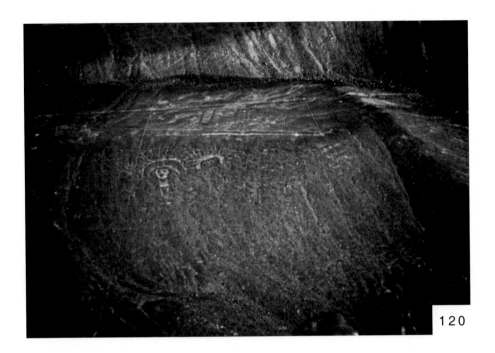

120

There the air force general Eduardo Jensen discovered the picture on a dry mountain slope above the Tarapaca desert in northern Chile. It is called the Atacama Giant. That's right! The figure is a full 121 meters high. (Images 124 and 125) The region of Tarapaca is part of the larger Atacama desert and the territory lies on a Chilean air force firing range. In years past, pilots used the Atacama Giant for target practice. That has in the meantime ceased. Like his double in Nazca, the head of the giant is equipped with "antennae" on both sides. The rectangular body is concluded at its lower end with a transverse beam. Be it in Nazca or Chile, the arms are angled in both cases and end in rough, plier-like grippers. Such duplication should really give archeologists cause for reflection, because the linear distance between Nazca and the firing range is 1,300 kilometers. But archeologists undertake their research in isolation and rarely transnationally. Their field of work is narrow and rarely intercontinental.

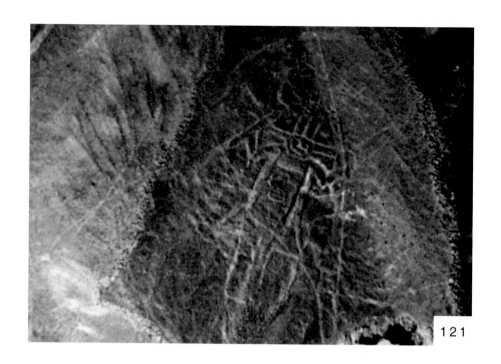

121

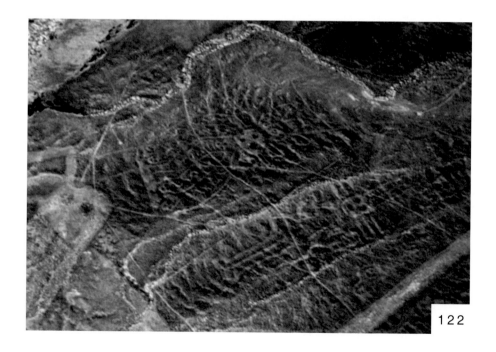

122

EVIDENCE OF THE GODS

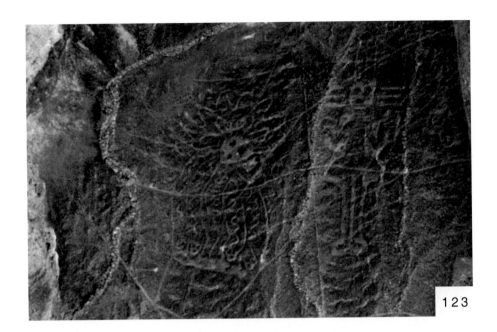

123

I have heard the objection that the Atacama Giant had been created in our time by ground personnel to make a fun target for the pilots. Total humbug! General Eduardo Jensen's discovery in August 1967 was a pure accident. He had flown along the steep coast in the early morning light and at first thought that he had seen an optical illusion. It required another two flights to confirm the find, which only becomes visible on the brown hillside under certain light conditions.

Another objection from amateurs, even if they are in possession of an archeological title, is beguiling but just as wrong: the Stone Age people of Nazca and Chile had copied their figures from old ceramic vessels. There are undoubtedly individual vessels with similar depictions as on the hillsides. What came first? The ceramics or the large depictions? If the ceramics came first, in which school did the motifs on them originate? And what means did the native people use to transform the small pictures on the vessels into the giants on the mountain sides? And why? The same applies with regard to textiles.

124

125

Symbols for Eternity

The Atacama desert in Chile (northwest of Antofagasta near the town of San Pedro de Atacama) might just as well be on Mars: dried up without a drop of water anywhere. There the mountain slopes are decorated with curious drawings that all stare up at the sky. For the native peoples, it must have been torture to create the figures in the burning heat. There are two squares with an arrow in the middle. It is pointing toward the earth with rungs like a ladder. (Image 126) Right next to it are symbols which, at first glance, look like writing. A message for the heavenly arrivals? Descend to us? (Images 127 and 128)

Or what about the "winged god with wheel" consisting of a wheel with spokes and below it two wings pointing down toward the earth? (Image 129) In between, there are rectangles, squares, animals...and they are not at all puny, but with side lengths of up to 20 meters. (Images 130 and 131) The two squares next to one another consisting of 12 smaller squares are also difficult to understand. A dual arrow runs down toward the earth from the right square. (Image 132) What was this message, which is only recognizable from the air, supposed to indicate? You will find us in the direction of the arrow? The question also applies with regard to the curved line that runs up a mountain slope and ends in a circle at its tip. (Image 133) Nothing but meaningless symbols to us—but they did mean something to those who created these messages. And these artistic minds were—and here we come to the crux of the matter—in similar mode worldwide. These symbols pointing toward the heavens are present in the desert soil of Majes and Sihuas in the Peruvian region of Arequipa, as much as in the Chilean region of Antofagasta. All made for the eyes of the gods. The same applies in the north in the extensive lava fields of the Mexican Sonora desert. There, too, we have the messages pointing upward. Farther north still, at the border between Mexico and California in the desert landscape of

126

Macahui, some bushes manage to grow; that is also the reason why the symbols on the ground were not discovered immediately. The area extends northward from the Tijuana-to-Mexicali road—at a point 25 kilometers from Mexicali heading toward Tijuana. (I am deliberately describing the geographical location in the hope that the younger generation will start searching for the clues. Nothing can be seen on Google Earth because of the bushes.) There, in an area that comprises at least 400 km², there are symbols on the ground which defy any explanation. There are circles, one next to the other, as far as the eye can see, as well as rectangles, half moons, wheels with several spokes, intertwined rings, and beings with radiating haloes. The diameters of the individual markings can reach up to 40 meters. But a warning for future researchers: the area lies on both sides of the border between the United States and Mexico. Permission must be sought at least from the U.S. border authorities. And there are dangerous poisonous snakes under the hot stones.

127

Still farther northward, not far from the little town of Blythe directly on the Colorado River, there are figures of people and animals that are up to 100 meters in size and which can only be seen from the air. (Images 134 and 135)

There can be no dispute: be it in South, Central, or North America, the native populations clearly operated a cult of mighty geoglyphs. Equally beyond dispute is the fact that the large majority of these geoglyphs are only recognizable from the air. Scientific work should look beyond its narrow local confines. Science normally looks for a common factor if there are several problems of the same kind. What is the common factor in all these geoglyphs? They are only recognizable to flying beings and have been created in areas in which they cannot be destroyed by flooding.

128

129

EVIDENCE OF THE GODS

130

131

132

133

EVIDENCE OF THE GODS

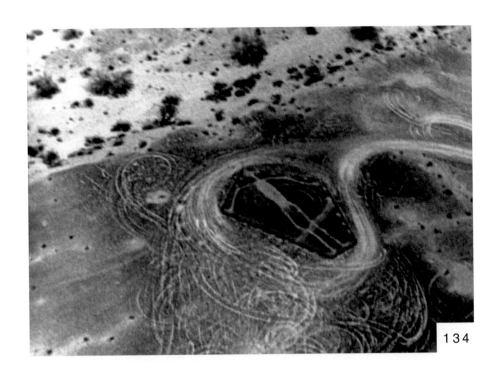

134

135

136

EVIDENCE OF THE GODS

Senseless Theories

Thus we are entitled to assume that our artistic ancestors around the world at least believed that someone "up there" would see their pictures. Smart alecks often accuse me of categorizing the people who lived thousands of years ago as not particularly intelligent. On the contrary, I consider them to be very clever. They were not so stupid as to lay down huge markings on the ground over generations without knowing that they would also actually be registered by some god or other. Which gods? All the gods that emerge from the psychological fog are of no use, because they would at best be relevant over only a narrowly restricted area. People for whom that is sufficient are welcome to look for the Nazca gods in Nazca—not in the Sonora desert! Let anyone who sees the indigenous Nazca people as being so restricted that they created their gigantic lines and markings for water gods be satisfied with that, but we can say with "divine certainty" that the water gods had nothing to do with the Atacama Giant in Chile. The rectangles scraped into the ground of the Nazca desert are "ceremonial sites," I read.[16] And what about the ones on the mountain slopes of San Pedro de Atacama? Scraped-out areas exist there too, only there is no opportunity for pious pilgrims to gather, because the slope is too steep, in addition to the horrific heat and the absence of any trails. Professor William Isbell argues in the journal *Spektrum der Wissenschaft* that the native Nazca people had scraped their symbols into the ground and on to the mountain slopes as "occupational therapy."[17] It strains credulity! Does "occupational therapy" not apply in other deserts, then? Or take Professor Helmut Tributsch, who saw a "Fata Morgana" behind the symbols.[18] That does not even apply to Nazca, let alone the Atacama desert.

And there is lots more in the same vein. A flood of academic nonsense, and each one of them is convinced of the correctness of his or her theory—indeed, considers it to be proven. Yet none

EVIDENCE OF THE GODS

137

of them can think outside the box. Rock drawings and large geoglyphs are a worldwide phenomenon which cannot be looked at in isolation. Even England boasts large figures on hillsides, such as the Cerne Abbas Giant or the 110-meter-long Uffington White Horse in Berkshire. (Images 136 and 137) Although the depictions in England look "modern" because the colors have been restored, they were nevertheless created in ancient times.

And They Did Fly!

The knockout argument put forward by the so-called serious authorities is always the same. After all, the sun, moon, and stars just happen to be located in the heavens, and therefore the naïve people had created symbols for these nature gods, they say. Anyone who advances those kind of arguments has no idea about ancient Indian culture,[19, 20] in which the flying machines of the gods are described in detail; knows nothing about what the Prophet Enoch said before the Great Flood,[21] who gives a first-person eyewitness account of his visit to the gods in the heavens; or has never heard anything about the *Kebra Nagast*.[22] Various airborne journeys of King Solomon are described there in the *Kebra Nagast*, including the speed with which the flying king was able to manage the great distances: "...thus Solomon covered a distance of three months in one day on his flying machine, without sickness and suffering, without hunger and thirst, without sweat and exhaustion. (*Kebra Nagast*, Chapter 58)

Arabia's most important geographer and encyclopedist, Al-Mas'udi (895–956) wrote in his *Histories* that Solomon had owned maps which showed "...the heavenly bodies, the stars, the earth with its continents and oceans, the inhabited regions, its plants and animals, and many other amazing things."[23] They did exist, these flying chariots of early times, and the people on the ground produced their large markings precisely for these flyers in the sky—a salute to heaven. The prehistoric pilots landed in various places. After all, they needed fresh food and water. In doing so, they were observed by the Stone Age people, who engraved the gods they did not understand into the rock walls. This happened worldwide, of course, because the flyers of antiquity were globally on the move in their airworthy crates. Their traces can be found everywhere.

In the fifth century, India's greatest poet, Kalidasa, lived at the court of the Gupta kings. In his epics, he draws on ancient Indian literature, to which he had access at the royal court. Thus he tells the story of the ancient rulers of Raghu in the *Raghuvamsa*, and in canto 13.1–79 there is a detailed and very precise account of a flight from Lanka to Ayodhya. There is a description of the panoramic view of the ocean from above, with its various depths, colors, and submarine mountains. The flying chariot sometimes flew between startled birds, then in the clouds, and even on paths "which are travelled by the gods." The regions and places over which the flight passes are precisely listed: "The Godavari River... the Agastya hermitage...Chitrakuta mountain near Allahabad and the cell of Atri on the Ganges...past the capital of the King of Nishada to the territory Uttarakoshala on the Sarayu River..." The people gathered on the ground watched the heavenly vehicle with astonishment from which Rama disembarked on steps of flashing metal.[24]

All in all, according to the description, the prehistoric journey by air covered a distance of 2,900 kilometers from Lanka (Ceylon) to Ayodhya, via Setubandha, Mysore, and Allahabad. When King Dushyanta came out of the aircraft, he noted to his surprise that although the wheels were turning, they did not stir up any dust. Furthermore, they did not touch the ground, although Rama emerged from the heavenly vehicle on metal steps. Matali, one of the pilots, enlightened the king: the difference was that, on this occasion, a heavenly vehicle of the gods had been used—and not one belonging to humans.

Precisely this remark highlights the essential difference. In those prehistoric times, there were a variety of flying machines: the flying crates of the human rulers and the high-tech flying vehicles of the gods, which were considerably more sophisticated than their earthly imitations. The mysterious Chi Kung people who built "flying chariots" for the founder of the Shang dynasty operated on the earth. The Indian King Rumanvat, who set off not only with his harem but also a crowd of dignitaries, engaged in human aviation, as did King Solomon and the Pacific god Rongomai. Selected, intelligent people were instructed by the gods in how to produce flying vehicles. That does not require any technical evolution or physical infrastructure. I could teach any Stone Age society how to make a hot air balloon and produce steam for a primitive drive. A propeller from hard wood would not represent any great feat either.

Any Other Questions?

The differences between "gods from space" and earthly kings, between flying chariots built by humans and the "heavenly designs," is clearly established in the ancient texts. Typical in this respect is Arjuna's journey to heaven. Arjuna is the hero of the story, and he flies off with Matali, the pilot. Even before they set off, Arjuna notices chariots that were lying on the ground unable to fly, as well as others hovering over the ground:

> ...Arjuna wished that Indra's heavenly chariot would come to him. And the chariot suddenly arrived in a blaze of light with Matali, driving darkness out of the air and illuminating the clouds, filling the regions of the world with noise, like thunder.... He joyously drove upward with the magic construct toward the sun-like chariot. When he neared the area invisible to mortals, inhabitants of earth, he saw

heavenly chariots of wondrous beauty, thousands of them. There the sun does not shine, nor the moon, there fire does not sparkle, but in their own brightness shine what are seen on earth as the stars. Because of the great distance, they do so look like lamps, although they are large bodies.[25]

I could really conclude this excursus about flying chariots—which, I am convinced, are the only reason for the giant markings on the ground and rock drawings of the gods (those with the rays)—with this comment: what more do you want? But cross-connections are like flashes of lightning in the memory. What was that about the heavenly vehicle? *"...filling the regions of the world with noise, like thunder...."* Just the same as in the Prophet Ezekiel in the Old Testament. There the noise of the heavenly chariot is compared with the noise of a host, the rushing and thunder of many waters. I know what that is about. After all, I have written 30 books on the subject.

And what did these "gods" actually want on earth? The answer is written in Chapter 11, verses 1–4 of the "Sabha Parva" (part of the Indian *Mahabharata*).[26] There it is reported that those gods had come in ancient times from a far distant place in space *to study human beings*. Interstellar ethnologists were at work.

But it was not just human beings who left rock drawings in honor of the gods and markings on the ground pointing toward the heavens. The gods themselves put a stamp on the earth's surface in a few places. Why on earth would they do that? It was probably for their heavenly "colleagues" or as messages for future generations. There might have been something important at specific locations to which the flying gentlemen wanted to draw the attention of other members of the airborne establishment.

Such messages can be viewed at a mountain slope near Palpa in Peru. Palpa is actually a part of the Nazca desert. The difference between Palpa and Nazca is academic more than anything else. In

138

Palpa, there is a rectangular "chessboard pattern" on the ground which only becomes visible under certain conditions of daylight. A second one extends from the first. (Image 138) Somehow the image is reminiscent of binary code. Then there is a giant "mandala," a geometric shape, whose message could never have been invented by Stone Age people. It was human hands which did the work—but under the guidance of a genius of geometry.

Sensation in Palpa

From the air, the first thing that becomes visible is a large circle with innumerable little dots on the circle line. In the middle, there are two superimposed rectangles divided into eight squares. (Image 139) These squares are subdivided by crossed lines and in the center there is a bundle of 16 lines raying out. The large geometrical figure is flanked on the right and left by two circles. The image as a whole produces a gigantic triangle consisting of three circles (two smaller ones and one larger one), a square, and the base lines around the geometrical message.

Why is this incredible image ignored in the specialist literature? Why do no mathematicians dare to think about the solution? It is claimed that the whole thing is a forgery created in our time. What led to that conclusion?

Two small wooden pegs were found at the edge of the mandala-like shape and dated using the C-14 method. The result suggested wood from our time. Case settled. Furthermore, someone had—intentionally?—left a small piece of cloth torn off some blue jeans lying about. That was sufficient for the supporters of the forgery theory. Sorry, friends from the other faculty: your rejection is premature.

In the 1960s, two teachers from Nazca attempted to measure out the mandala, which has been resting in the ground for an eternity, in order to draw a copy. They stumbled about the burning-hot stone desert with small sections of branch. The string for making the measurements was to be attached to the wood. The work was soon abandoned. The task was too enormous and too complicated. Today such measurements could be undertaken from the air.

The proportions of the whole diagram argue against a forgery. All three circles in the triangle have a side length of several hundred meters. Furthermore, and this is something that the critics should really have noticed, an ancient cut in the terrain runs right through the middle of the image. (Image 140) It starts at the edge of the inner rectangle, widens, goes through the inner and outer circle and beyond the frame of the encompassing square. Here—and this is the crucial point!—the circle and lines also pass through the cut in the terrain. For the unknown creators of the diagram, that seems not to have mattered—for today's forgers, in contrast, it would have represented a serious problem.

It is true that there are figures and messages in Peru which originate in our time, including in the area around Nazca and

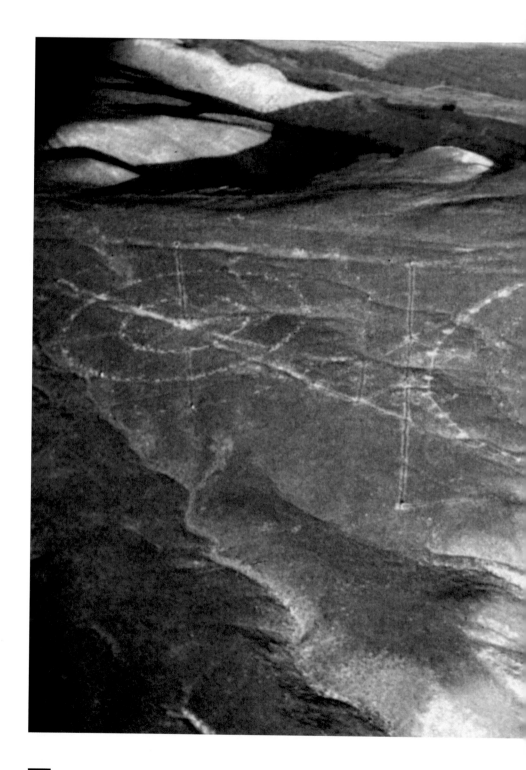

EVIDENCE OF THE GODS

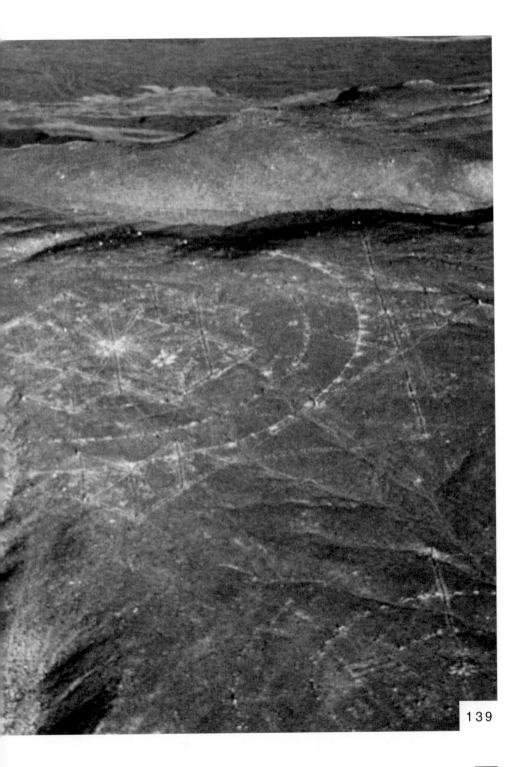

139

EVIDENCE OF THE GODS

140

141

Palpa—for example, the emblems or initials of political parties. But they are created in places which are easy to reach, not on mountain slopes with cuts in the terrain.

A precise study of the geometric depiction on the high plateau supports the genuine nature of the shape. To the right and left of the large square in the middle, there are circles consisting of an outer and inner ring each. At the center of each, a star can be seen with a central point and eight lines raying out. (Image 141) From this center point, a long, straight line goes to the two smaller circles on the right and the left. This line also goes over the cut in the terrain. The extension ends in the "Nazca piste" (not visible on the picture). The center of the large circle also forms a point from which lines ray out, with two overlapping rectangles. Then there is an inner and an outer ring. The stones of the inner ring run both through the cut in the terrain and a hollow. I took the trouble to count the points in so far as possible. In the inner ring, there are about 90 points, in the outer about 63.

The superimposed rectangles in the center of the large circle are, in turn, bisected by lines which precisely intersect the corner points of the square in the middle. The whole structure is a masterpiece of geometry. Furthermore—just like the chessboard pattern—the geometric message is embedded in the Nazca network.

The Forgery That Isn't

Just imagine that forgers today had produced the geometric message. The first question is, What for? Well, maybe to make Nazca and Palpa more attractive for tourists. Tourists are flown over Nazca daily in small aircraft. But the thing that the pilots precisely do *not* do is fly their guests over the mandala and chessboard pattern, because they are not part of the scraped out drawings of Nazca at all. All that forgery for nothing? Friends, the matter is more complicated than might appear at first sight: both the mandala (the large geometric creation) and the chessboard pattern only become visible if approached from the air at a particular angle. If the pilot approaches from the wrong angle or height, the structure does not exist. In a complex piece of work, several geometric points would have to have been fixed and marked with string before work started. The boss of the team of forgers would need to be a geometry professor and his gang prepared to gather stones into huge triangles, circles, and rectangles for weeks in the burning heat. All that sweat-soaked effort just for a forgery? No one goes voluntarily into hell, not even the members of the Peruvian army. Furthermore, they would have arrived in all-terrain vehicles. Finally, the work gang would sweat off a large quantity of water. Where are the tracks of the vehicles? Where the paths of the industrious forgers?

If a clique of forgers had been at work in Nazca/Palpa in our time, such months of effort would most certainly not have gone unnoticed. Where are the triumphant sensational reports in the local press? We did it!

142

143

EVIDENCE OF THE GODS

When I flew over Nazca and Palpa each evening in the autumn of 1996, I asked Eduardo, the chief pilot of Nazca at the time, "Who scraped these forgeries into the ground? Who gathered the stones?"

"That is no modern forgery! That thing has always been here!"

"Why don't any of the many Nazca reporters write about it? I can't remember having seen a picture of it."

Eduardo, the oldest pilot at the time, informed me that, first, the diagram was not located on the plain of Nazca but in Palpa and, second, no one knew what to say about it. All that remained was a big silence.

That has not changed to the present day. Neither the geometric message nor the chessboard pattern are discussed anywhere. Not even the young pilots who today fly tourists over Nazca know what is correct. Hardly any of them even know of the geometric drawings. That does not surprise me. After all, they can only be seen under certain conditions of light and angles of approach. So the younger pilots think, with a shrug of the shoulders, that it is probably a forgery while the older ones maintain that the geometry has always been there, but has hardly been noticed because of the light conditions. No one wants to burn their fingers. No one dares to refute the loud claims of forgery. But they *can* be refuted. How?

Image 142 shows a section of the smaller accompanying ring on the right. Two straight lines cross the center and extend beyond the outer ring. Part of the line which frames the large mandala in the center can be seen to the left of the picture. The twin tracks of this line can be seen clearly in the picture. The alleged forgers would therefore not only have taken the trouble to frame the central representation with a square, but they would also have drawn the white line of this square twice—totally daft for forgers. They do not create extra work for nothing.

Image 143 shows a close-up outside the central depiction. We can still barely recognize strange rectangular shapes on the ground,

144

145

EVIDENCE OF THE GODS

which move outward from a point in a star shape. One line of the Nazca network runs toward it and touches the central mandala. So the "forgery" somehow belongs to the complex of lines of Nazca. In whatever form, flying planners were at work.

Image 144 is not about the geometric figures but about the surrounding terrain. Where is the car park for the vehicles of the forgers with their water barrels? They would not even have been able to ascend the steep slope on the right at the front (lower edge of picture). Where are the tire tracks? How and why would one plant an incredible geometric shape on a section of land which cannot be seen from anywhere, except when approached from the air in a particular direction? Why undertake the exercise in a dried-out desert when no human soul would ever see this magnificent stroke of genius? Forgers who produce a work like that want an audience, admirers, and applause for their achievement. All markings from our time—political messages, for example—are located on hillsides near roads with traffic, such as the famous Pan-American Highway, the route from Alaska to Tierra del Fuego. It runs through the deserts of Nazca/Palpa. Yet the geometric miracle lies completely off any road in a burning hell hostile to any humans. Where is the signature of the genius forger? I have heard the objection that it sometimes rains violently for a brief period in Nazca/Palpa. The downpours should have washed the shapes away a long time ago if they were actually old. Not true. The same rain would have made the shapes, pistes, and zig-zag lines on the plain of Nazca/Palpa disappear. But that did not happen.

The chessboard pattern consists of more than 800 individual points, though they cannot be counted precisely. Just as with the mandala, a kind of water course runs transversely across the pattern here too. (Image 145) Should the rare rain water not have made these points disappear a long time ago as well if they were old? Precisely not. Why? Several undisputed old lines run their course to the left of the chessboard pattern. Irritatingly, they do so just as directly across water courses as those in the chessboard pattern. Any rainfalls were not able to wash away these definitively old lines at all. They exist beyond dispute. The fourth and fifth from the left even run for two meters in the water course. No trace of wearing away. The proponents of the forgery theory should think again. And the question about the tire tracks is also resolved under the magnifying glass: there aren't any, neither on the first nor the second chessboard pattern.

It seems to me that a discussion of the geometric figures is not wanted, hence the moaning about forgeries—nothing unusual about that in our society. The spirit of the times only permits what is reasonable. And a geometric message from the past cannot exist. Period! Anyone who speaks about it is unreasonable. Who, actually, can protect us from reasonable people?

Giant Salute!

In fact, I can produce even more impressive pictures, whether the spirit of the times likes it or not. In Ica, a provincial capital 140 kilometers north of Nazca/Palpa, a giant salutes the heavens from a rocky plateau. Image 146 is the original; in Image 147, we have outlined the contours. The monster has broad feet angled outward and long legs, and its left arm is held at an angle. The head has been destroyed and the right arm appears to hold a long object. What is that all about? Another forgery? This time the figure was not laid out with stones but chiseled directly into the rock. Not in this and not in the last century. Anyone who argues that the Giant of Ica, as the figure is known, is not pointing at the heavens probably cannot cope with the message to the gods.

Even in Nazca, among the tangle of lines, a 29-meter-high figure generally called El Astronauta, "the astronaut," is stuck to a hillside. (Image 148) The skull is dominated by two round eyes, the proportions of the body are correct, and the feet appear to be wearing heavy shoes. The arms are remarkable: one arm is pointing

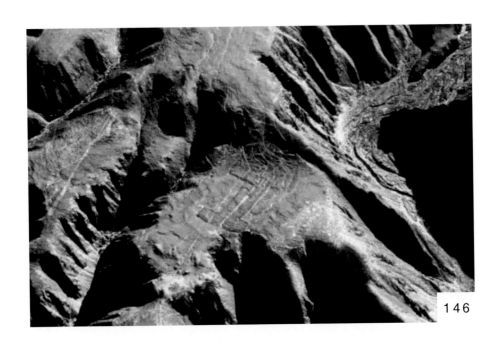

146

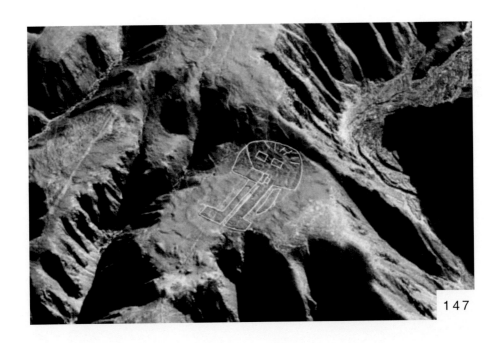

147

148

149

EVIDENCE OF THE GODS

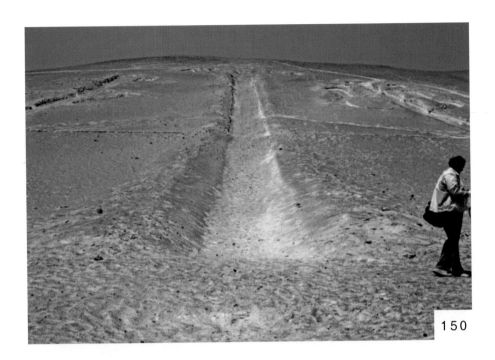

150

toward the sky, the other toward the earth. Is this intended to signal the connection of Heaven–Earth? (Incidentally, the whirling dervishes in Turkey, who rotate their body at great speed in their flowing robes, point one arm at the earth and the other at the sky, with the intention of indicating the connection between heaven and earth.) El Astronauta in Nazca is framed by two vertical lines. There must originally have been other figures on the same hill. Their contours can only just still be recognized. And there is a surprising three-dimensional effect which only becomes visible when the sun is low. Suddenly El Astronauta appears to step out of the hill.

The next symbol which has not been understood lies in the Bay of Pisco, Peru, directly on the Pacific coast. The shape is reminiscent of a huge trident or a gigantic three-armed candelabra. (Image 149) The structure as a whole measures a full 250 meters in

151

height, and the individual pillars of the trident are up to 3.8 meters wide. (Image 150) The substrate consists of a white, salt-like, and crystalline substance. (Image 151) In earlier years, I scrambled up the sandy slope with small groups of people to take close-up photos and make measurements. In doing so, we left masses of footprints. Yet the next day, our footprints were literally gone with the wind. Nothing—nothing at all—indicated that we had ever been there. Today, entering the Candelabro—as the figure is known locally—is prohibited. No one knows what the structure means, who created it, and when it was done. The logical explanation would actually be that the mark is a sign for shipping. But even that is controversial, because there is a small island off the coast, which is only inhabited by roaring and smelly sea lions. This island blocks the view from the sea, and also from the north and the south, one can only look into the Bay of Pisco from a few kilometers away. Furthermore, the island itself would be the best mark for shipping. It can be seen from a long distance away, while the Candelabro only appears once the island has been passed. I have read somewhere that the Candelabro points to the lines on the plain of Nazca about 100 kilometers away. Wrong. The central arm does not point to Nazca. In any event, the shape fits into the picture of symbols pointing heavenward on the Pacific coast.

The Avenue of Pockmarks

What starts as an asphalt road runs from the Bay of Pisco into the Pisco Valley to Humay. The road turns into a dusty gravel track up into the Andes to Castrovirreyna and Huancavelica. Fruit and vegetables grow where fields can be irrigated with water piped to sprinklers. The sudden transition from desert to cultivated landscape is jolting. The Hacienda Montesierpe lays to the right of the track, and next to it is a small chapel. Behind the hacienda, there is an approximately 300-meter-wide strip of cultivated land on the hillside which is artificially irrigated. Another 200 meters farther on, there is one hole after another in the dry soil of the slope. Widthwise, there are always eight holes next to one another. Each hole is about one meter deep and of the same width. (Image 152) And each hole has remnants of a wall. No matter whether you look up or down the mountain, the "ticker tape" is always visible. It is like a tapeworm or as if a scarifier precisely eight spikes wide had been rolled up and down the hill. (Image 153) The width of the band is about 24 meters, the length could not be determined.

I crawled up the slope as far as possible—often on all fours. Sometimes the holes were porous, the stone crumbling, but the higher I climbed the more small walls surrounded the holes. (Images 154 and 155) What could that be? A former tree nursery? A kind of cemetery? A defensive position? The border of sovereign territory?

The cemetery variant did not make any sense. Bones, ceramics, or textiles have never been found here. A tree nursery or plantation of some other kind was also out of the question. The ticker tape ran up and down the mountain often at a sloping angle and there was no water in any case. So a defensive system? Useless. Any attacker could have come from both sides; the defenders would have been shooting at one another. Furthermore, the ticker tape ran across a slope which dropped off steeply to the right and left. The defenders could neither have escaped nor been given reinforcement. The strip often nestles in the slope, gently winding its way downward and across the valley. If the holes were something like one-man bunkers, the defenders would often have been positioned lower than the advancing attackers. There was no logic to it, no simple solution made any sense. The native inhabitants have for centuries called the strip "la avenida misteriosa de las picaduras de viruelas"— the mysterious avenue of pockmarks.

From the air, the "ticker tape" looks like the track of a tracked vehicle which scrambled up and down the mountain here. But no such tracked vehicle exists anywhere. Then take the idea of a snake. Who was going to engrave a snake on to the slopes? A snake which slithers down the mountain, across the valley, and then up again?

152

153

EVIDENCE OF THE GODS

154

Serpents and Mica

I do not want to exclude anything, because the Native Americans of North America, at least, have placed depictions of animals of all kinds on their hills. There are artificially created mounds showing birds, bison, bears, lizards, and snakes. The pictures are only recognizable as complete works of art from the air. In the state of Ohio in the United States, between the capital city, Columbus, and Newark, there is a gigantic rectangle. Nearby, in Adams County west of the town of Portsmouth, there is the Great Serpent Mound. The geoglyph is a good 400 meters long, and for its whole length, nuzzles the bends of Bush Creek—albeit a good 40 meters above the water. (Image 156) The head of the snake rests on the highest point of the hilly terrain, the body winds its way for the whole 400 meters like an endless serpent, finally terminating in a spiral. Local

156

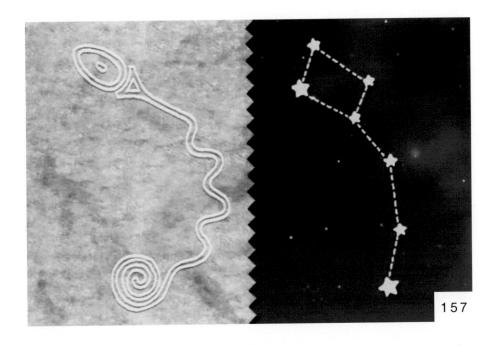

157

158

legend has it that Great Serpent Mound is a depiction of the constellation Ursa Minor, the Small Bear. (Image 157)

A grave mound with various small bones was discovered at the lower end of the serpent. They were lying on a layer of mica. (Image 158) Mica is a potassium aluminum hydrosilicate which is found in granite mountains. The substance sparkles in the sun and has both elasticity and tensile strength. Mica can resist temperatures of up to 800 degrees Centigrade and is resistant to all organic acids. The characteristics of mica are very much in demand today because mica is an excellent electrical insulator. It is also resistant against arcing and electrical discharges. Sheets of mica can be separated like turning the pages of a book. (Image 159) I keep being aggravated by the puzzling parallels between places which are far apart. A thick layer of mica was also discovered in Teotihuacan. The place is 40 kilometers distant from Mexico City. There, only a few meters away from

159

160

161

EVIDENCE OF THE GODS

162

the Avenue of the Dead, an underground chamber was discovered which had been insulated with mica. (Images 160, 161, and 162) All of this was done an unknown time ago—both Tiahuanaco/Mexico and the Great Serpent Mound in Ohio. My question is not why native tribes far apart from one another did the same thing. It happened in rock drawing as well, after all. I am aggravated for another reason: the native inhabitants must have known about the multiple properties of mica. Otherwise, they would neither have used it nor mined it in far-distant granite mountains. This would not have been a simple matter.

The danger when looking for new explanations is that you might actually find them.

163

164

EVIDENCE OF THE GODS

Chapter 3

STONES

CAN

TALK

_____

I once learned in high school that our ancestors—only recently descended from the apes—vegetated in caves, groomed each other's fur for lice, hunted mammoth or other animals from time to time, and otherwise chewed on berries and roots. Maybe so. But another group of the Stone Age family behaved in a highly intellectual way. Its mathematic and geometric performance shows that. No doubt about it! I constantly hear scientists demanding facts. They would respond positively to facts. Which scientists? It is really the responsibility of "Paleolithic specialists." But they can be counted on the fingers of one hand and are, furthermore, geographically fixated. They restrict themselves to a particular area. The framework of their thinking follows evolution. Higher geometry, for example, has no place in the Stone Age. As a wanderer between the sciences, I learned a long time ago that facts are also filtered, that they are bent and squeezed until suddenly everything fits again and we can return to the same old things. However, the monuments from the Stone Age—stone circles, dolmens, menhirs, for example—are found just as much across a range of countries as rock drawings and geoglyphs. It appears there must have been some kind of prehistoric tourism in which the sages traveled from tribe to tribe and passed on their tidings. In Central America, and this is generally known, the Maya built pyramids and temples in accordance with astronomical principles. In that respect, scholars refer to a "magic imperative" of calendar and astronomy. What was the situation in Europe at a time, furthermore, long *before* Central America? What "magic imperative" caused the Stone Age tribes to do the same thing? Who taught them the Pythagorean theorem, the number pi, the pentagram, and other achievements of mental geometry? Why did they all have the idea of aligning their mass graves astronomically and building huge stone or wood circles? The proof of my claims is available. It can be checked, photographed, measured—as demanded by high-flown science. Yet no one is interested. Any documentation just produces a confused shake of the head. What do we prefer? To adjust our thinking or to continue to live with a product that has passed its sell-by date?

In the Gulf of Morbihan in Brittany, France, not far from the town of Carnac with its thousands of menhirs (stone columns), there are two small green islands: Gavrinis and Er Lannic. The tiny island of Er Lannic has the remains of a stone circle, or more precisely a slight oval, of between 58 and 49 meters diameter, consisting of 49 megaliths. Only half of these stones are positioned on land; the other half is submerged by the tides. (Images 163 and 164) In the same location, almost 9 meters deeper, there is a second stone circle consisting of 33 blocks. They can just be recognized at low tide during a calm sea. The two stone rings merge like a figure of eight. The circle under water has a diameter of 65 meters.

Flooding? No, the water has risen. When? About 18,000 years ago. How do we know that?

Underwater Rock Drawings

One September morning in 1985, Monsieur Henri Cosquer, an employee of a diving school in Cassis (east of Marseille, France) dived into the depths off Cape Morgiou. He was not actually looking for anything in particular—other than to admire the wonders of the sea. At a depth of 35 meters, directly next to a small rockslide, Henri Cosquer noticed the entrance to a cave and cautiously swam into it. The diver quickly realized that the cave led to an ascending underwater tunnel. On that morning, Henri Cosquer did not dare to go further. Time was limited; he only had enough oxygen for another half hour. Also, he had neither underwater lights nor a camera with him.

A few weeks later, Henri Cosquer tried again in the same spot. This time his diver friends Marc and Bernhard were with him, and the diving equipment was also more professional than what he had at the first attempt. The men carefully swam through a 40-meter-long corridor and finally reached the surface in an underground lake. Their searchlights illuminated an incredible scene. They recognized two horses on the western wall of a chamber. Bernhard's searchlight flitted to the ceiling and alighted on a goat drawn in black charcoal. It was covered by a transparent calcite layer. Now the men clambered out of the water, took off their flippers, and checked the air in the subterranean chambers. It was spicy and a little resinous, but could be breathed without difficulty. In the next chamber, even larger than the first one, the light beams skimmed over a whole picture gallery: bison, penguins, cats, antelopes, a seal, and various geometric symbols.

Henri Cosquer showed his photos to some archeologists. They were not very enthusiastic, remained skeptical, or even thought that the pictures were forgeries. It was not until six years later, on September 19, 1991, that the *Archéonaut*, a French naval research vessel, anchored off Cape Morgiou. Eleven frogmen followed Henri

Cosquer into the cave system. Eight specialists were waiting aboard the *Archéonaut*, including two archeologists. Specialist equipment was lowered into the depths, the subterranean picture gallery was thoroughly mapped, and small samples of the paintings were brought to the surface. The C-14 dating produced a minimum age of 18,400 years.

Climate Change

The sea level of the Mediterranean 18,400 ago was 35 meters lower than today. At that time, the entrance to the cave was on land. The water has risen—be it in the Mediterranean or in the Atlantic at Er Lannic. That can also be proved at the port of Lixus in Morocco, where the oldest parts lie under water; at Cadiz in Spain, where a 100-meter-long piece of road can still be seen underwater at low tide; in Malta, where so-called "cart ruts" sink below the surface of the Mediterranean; and off the island of Bimini in the Caribbean, where clear remains of walls and a road lie under the surface of the sea. The sea has risen—worldwide. It's as simple as that. (There are many other examples of water having risen. Even Plato wrote about it some 2,500 years ago, in the third book of his *Laws*.)

Today, as I'm sitting typing these words on my keyboard, mankind is being gripped by an unfathomable debate: climate change. The glaciers are said to be melting and the oceans rising. But they have been doing that every few thousand years, quite obviously also in the Stone Age, when there were no industrially produced CO_2 waste gases to warm the climate. What is wrong with this society? Looking the other way, spreading ignorance and half-truths, not taking account of the facts—the same also applies to many scientists, particularly the type who constantly and angrily demand to be taken seriously. That is the society we live in. Looking away and refusing to register what is also applies to the incredible messages from the Stone Age.

165

The small island of Gavrinis lies directly next to the two stone circles of Er Lannic, which are partly disintegrating under the water. Before the sea level rose, Gavrinis and Er Lannic were part of the landmass. Gavrinis is a mere 750 meters long and 400 meters wide. The island is fringed by trees. Mossy grass and rampantly proliferating gorse cushions one's steps, as if a thick carpet had been laid down leading into the sacred place. And what a sacred place it is! For the "passage grave" on the hillock has been fitted with a mathematical message which can turn us smart-alecks speechless.

The indigenous Bretons always knew that the hillock in truth contained a structure from the Stone Age. The entrance was discovered in 1832—the apparent grave inside was empty—and between 1979 and 1984, an archeological team led by Dr. Charles-Tanguy Le Roux restored the cyclopean complex. The inside of the passage grave turned out to be a phantom from a time long past and, at the same time, contained the most logical of all answers: mathematics.

168 EVIDENCE OF THE GODS

166

167

The Stone Agers began by completely flattening the hill on the island of Gavrinis. Then they carted huge quantities of stones of various sizes to the building site and also rolled a few dozen cyclopic megaliths along. (Image 165) Even the floor of the passage grave consists of slabs. The builders must have known from the beginning that they were creating a message for eternity.

The entrance consists of two vertical stone slabs with a horizontal one on top. (Image 166) This is followed by a gallery, flanked and covered by monoliths, into the interior of the artificial hill. (Image 167) Then there is the "sanctum," also called the "burial chamber," although a grave has never been found. This "burial chamber" is a further 2.6 meters long, 2.5 meters wide, and 1.8 meters high. It is formed by six mighty slabs and covered by a gigantic ceiling slab which measures 3.7 by 2.5 meters. In total, 52 megaliths were

168

169

used to build the actual passage grave, of which half (26) were engraved with strange symbols. The local archeologists assume that these ornaments were carved deep into the stone slabs with small quartz stones. Logically this work would have had to be done while the slabs were still lying on the ground, that is before the passage grave was built. That is the first thing to make us prick up our ears. The people who built this masterpiece cannot have been pottering about in a piecemeal fashion, in whatever way happened to work best at the time, but they must have been working to plan. They knew in advance which engraved slab later had to be placed in which position. The engravings are of innumerable spirals and circles which flow into and over one another, peculiar grooves which look like enlarged fingerprints, snaking lines which often flow over from one monolith to another, and in all this confusion a slab with depictions which are reminiscent of axes or pointed rock implements. (Images 168–172) It is an engraved world which, depending on the angle of the light, throws bizarre shadows on the curious patterns on the walls. It is these grooves which speak. They contain the mathematical message, timeless and valid for every generation that can do sums.

170

171

EVIDENCE OF THE GODS

172

Math Exercise in Stone

The mathematics were discovered by Mr. Gwenc'hlan Le Scouëzec, a Breton and obviously a mathematical genius, although he modestly thinks that the thousands-of-years-old message is quite obvious to everyone.[1]

The count begins where everything has to start in mathematics, with one. Counting from the entrance, the sixth stone on the right is particularly conspicuous. It is smaller than all the others and is engraved with a single "fingerprint"—nothing to the side or on top, only the circles and grooves of a "fingertip." It is the only stone with just a single symbol. All the others either have no engravings at all or several at once. Does the sixth stone indicate the number 6? Was this intended to signal the system which was to be used for the calculation?

The 21st stone in the gallery shows a "fingerprint" at the bottom, above which there are three rows, one above the other, with a total of 18 ax-like, vertical engravings. (Image 173) Eighteen is equivalent to 3 × 6. The multiplication of 3 × 4 × 5 × 6 gives 360 or 60 × 6. The 18, the number of "axes," in turn signals the twentieth part of 360. In our geometric system, this number represents the number of degrees in a full circle. But what is the connection between our system and the past?

Three, four, five, and six written in sequence read as 3456. This figure is present on the 21st monolith. 3456 divided by 21 gives 164.57. This, in turn, is the circumference of a circle with a diameter of 52.38 meters. So what? Why all the fooling about? The southern azimuth on the day of the summer solstice for the position of Gavrinis is precisely 52 degrees 38 minutes. Do I still need to mention that the passage grave is of course aligned with the solstitial point? Can things become any more confusing? Oh yes, they can. These coincidences are only the beginning. We only divided the

173

number 3456 by 21 because it appears on the 21st monolith. The result was 164.57. That turned out to be a circle with a diameter of 52.38 meters. What happens when we divide the two numbers? Grab your calculator; it has to be $164.57 \div 52.38 = 3.14$. The famous number pi.

Pure chance, the skeptics cry, and numbers can prove anything. They are right, but in the case of Gavrinis, chance is excluded. The engravings keep indicating, to anyone willing to see, how to proceed or which numbers to use for division. Image 174 shows the "ax" and to its left indicates the number to be used for division. The number of monoliths and their position was also intentional:

a. The right side of the passage has 12 slabs.

b. The "burial chamber" has six slabs.

c. The left side of the passage has 11 slabs.

The two numbers in a + b fit into the pattern, because adding them gives 18 and that is the number of "axes" engraved on the 21st monolith. But what about the monoliths on the left side of the passage? The number 11 does not fit into a series of six in any way.

One moment, please! The recurring basic figure was 3456. Divide this number by 11, because of the 11 monoliths on the left side. The result once again is the pi number 314.18. If we place a point between 3456 and divide 34.56 by 11, we can of course only get the result 3.14.

And it keeps going on like that. Gwenc'hlan Le Scouëzec has demonstrated it beyond dispute in his comprehensive work *Bretagne Megalithique*. Gavrinis turns out to be a treasure trove of numbers, in which three different, mutually independent calculation systems are integrated which can, however, be combined: a senary system with its multiples, a decimal system, and a base 52 system with the sub-magnitude 26. (The Mayan calendar is based on the base 52 system.) The senders of the numerical message of Gavrinis thought

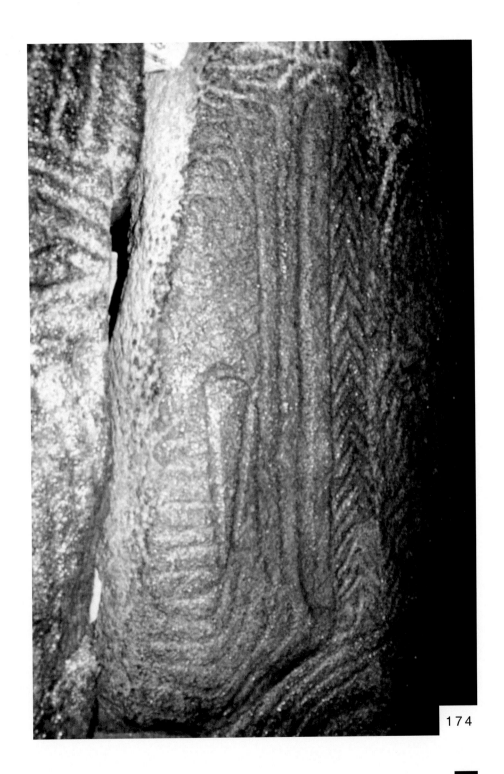

174

of everything. No matter in which calculation system future generations would be working, they could not avoid stumbling on the solution, whatever the case. The Pythagorean theorems are also integrated into the mass of data of Gavrinis—long before Pythagoras!—as well as the number for the synodic lunar orbit (down to the decimal point!), the spherical shape of the earth together with its diameter, as well as the length of the earth year at 365.25 days.

Gwenc'hlan Le Scouëzec, who cracked the mathematical code of Gavrinis, concluded his considerable achievement with the words: "It is quite possible that in the many calculations some are less certain than others which are truly of key significance. On the other hand, there are too many coincidences for the key common features to have arisen by chance."[2]

All just gimmickry and random chance? Before I add examples from the Stone Age, which have nothing to do with number games but only with astronomy, I wish to make the point that the passage grave of Gavrinis was created fully intentionally for recipients in the far distant future. First the Stone Agers leveled the site, then they carted thousands of stones there, cut the monoliths for the floor and ceiling slabs to size, and chiseled the engravings *before construction*. Once the work was done, they covered the artificial hill with sand and earth, so that grass and bushes would grow on it. The megaliths prevented the interior from being damaged. In the far distant future, human beings would notice that the hill did not fit into the landscape. We *have* noticed. The message has arrived.

The next example has nothing to do with numbers but with the relationship between the earth and the sun.

175

A 5,000-Year-Old Miracle

For the last 5,165 years—calculated backward from 2012—to the present day, the same miracle has taken place in Ireland each year. It happens once again in a "passage grave"—although here, too, a corpse has never materialized. The place is called Newgrange, and it lies 51 kilometers northwest of Dublin or about 15 kilometers west of the town of Drogheda. There, in the county of Meath, in a loop of the river Boyne, the original inhabitants of Ireland set a grandiose memorial into the landscape. It is a technical miracle from the Stone Age. It is not simply a grave surrounded by stones to prevent animals getting at the corpse. Newgrange is a masterpiece of surveying, a lesson in astronomy, and a transport phenomenon. It was built at a time when, according to orthodox archeological opinion, Egyptian history had not yet happened, there was no pyramid on earth, and the cities of Ur, Babylon, or Knossos did

176

not yet exist. Presumably the impressive stone circle of Stonehenge had not yet been planned when unknown astronomers built the passage grave of Newgrange.

For thousands of years, no one paid attention to the round hill above the river Boyne, until in 1699, when the road worker Edward Lhwyd swore mightily. A boulder blocking the line of the road would not budge. When it had been half-freed from the earth, the swearing road worker noticed two engraved spirals and some rectangles on the recalcitrant block. Now everything became clear: "Another one of those damned graves." The message reached the next pub. Newgrange had been discovered. (Image 175)

Thorough excavations did not begin until the 1960s. In 1969, the lead researcher Professor Michael J. O'Kelly from Cork University discovered a right-angled artificial opening above the two monoliths at the entrance. It was only 20 centimeters wide, but

that was enough for the scholar to see the light. (Image 176) On the day of the winter solstice in 1969—and again one year later—O'Kelly seated himself right at the back of the vault. Here is his eye-witness account:

> Exactly at 9:45, the upper edge of the sun appeared on the horizon, and at 9:58 the first shaft of direct sunlight appeared through the small roofbox above the entrance. The beam of sunlight then lengthened along the passage into the burial chamber until the beam reached the edge of the basin stone in the niche. When the beam of light had widened into a 17-centimeter ribbon and flooded the floor of the chamber, the reflection illuminated the grave so dramatically that various details both of the side chambers and of the vaulted roof could be clearly seen. At 10:04 the ribbon of light began to narrow and precisely at 10:25 the beam of light was abruptly cut off. So for 21 minutes at sunrise on the shortest day of the

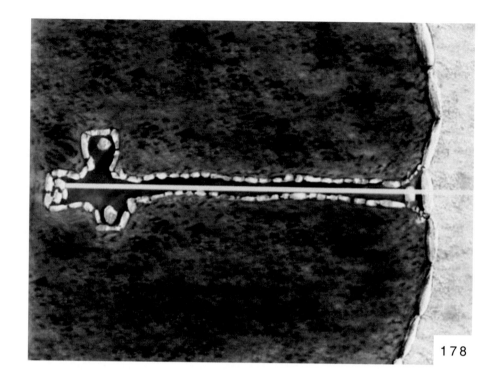

178

year sunlight penetrates directly into the burial chamber of Newgrange. Not through the entrance but through a specially constructed narrow slit above the entrance to the passage.[3] (Images 177 and 178)

As a cautious academic, Professor O'Kelly did not at the time want to give a final answer to the question whether the light show was accidental or intended. The question has meanwhile been ticked off by others.[4]

Planned Lightshow

The two Irish scientists Tom Ray and Tim O'Brian from the School of Cosmic Physics set up their instruments in the burial chamber on December 21, 1988. Precisely 4.5 minutes after sunrise, the first beam of light appeared in the rectangular opening above the entrance. After a short period, the shaft of light widened into a 34 centimeter ribbon which was however—horror of horrors!—abruptly reduced to 26 centimeters by a slightly inclined monolith. (Image 179) The chamber was still illuminated, but no longer to the full width of the original beam. What had happened?

Tom and Tim set their computers to work. In the course of the millennia, the earth's axis performs a slow wobble, as a consequence of which "east" 5,000 years ago was not precisely where it is now. But 5,134 years ago—the computer calculations say—the full width of the sunbeam had lit up the vault through the opening in precise alignment with the compass and had unfolded its lightshow on the rear wall at a distance of 24 meters. Even taking account of the wobble in the earth's axis, there is little change in the lightshow. The only factor to influence the light beam today is the slightly inclined monolith. Random chance was excluded. The builders of Newgrange had planned the magic lightshow. Now some questions need answering.

The position of a single monolith in the passage would have changed everything. If the artificial slit over the entrance had been a few centimeters smaller, or if its position had been a few millimeters off, the fingers of light could not have reached the back wall through the passage and chamber. Furthermore, had the passage of monoliths been shorter or longer, the sunlight would either not have reached the back wall or not illuminated the cultic symbols. With a shorter passage, the light beam would have fizzled out on the ground due to the slope of the terrain.

There is more: The giant complex of Newgrange is not set on even ground, and the east-west passage does not lie horizontally but slopes upward. The highest point on the floor of the passage is also the location of the last monolith after 24 meters. This angle of ascent was planned. The starting point of the sunbeams on December 21

179

180

was not the entrance of the grave, nor did the beams creep from the floor at the entrance to the back, but they entered through a small rectangular opening above the entrance monoliths. This position alone, in combination with the hill lying opposite behind which the sun rose, allowed for a straight beam of light into the center of the vault.

There the light hit the edge of the "basin stone," a block with an artificially scraped out basin, like a bundled laser beam. What came next was a magic symphony, triggered through the mirror effect of the basin stone. The beams fanned out in various directions, always directed at cultic symbols and, of course, at a right angle straight upward like an arrow through the shaft of the vaulted roof. (Image 180)

This vault over the passage grave is a marvel in itself. Specialists call it a *corbel vault*. Heavier monoliths below and lighter monoliths above were placed on top of one another in such a way that the next

181

highest monolith always extended a little over the edge of the one below. This created a six-meter high steadily narrowing hexagonal shaft over the center of the grave. At the top of the chimney, the gap was bridged with a flat stone which could be removed as required. (Image 181)

Compelling Conclusions

Slogans have a stronger echo in empty vaults. Why must Newgrange have been a grave? The grave idea haunts the specialist literature as a fact and can probably never be eliminated. What are these facts? Human and animal bones were found in Newgrange, *ergo* the complex has been built for that purpose. It is also a fact that every dugout, every convenient hole, can be used as a grave—even if *originally* it served a completely different purpose. In the same way, the idea for Newgrange might have been a completely different one even if—much later—bones were added. The rest of the dead was deemed to be sacred among all peoples, so only the bones in the vault of Newgrange were to be startled and blinded by the sun each year? If Newgrange was conceived as a grave complex from the very beginning, then the deceased person must have had a very special affinity with our central star. If not, the rectangular opening for the shafts of sunlight does not make any sense.

No tribe can manage a cultic structure like Newgrange as a spare-time job. An observation and surveying period of at least one generation was the prerequisite for determining the day, hour, and minute of the winter solstice for the geographical situation of Newgrange. Precise plans or models had to be made, every angle on the *inclined* building site had to be correctly aligned, the position of every individual monolith had to be exactly correct, and of course the cultic stones with their geometric engravings had to be anchored in the tunnel before the complex was closed off. Oh yes, and before the actual building work, the hill had to be removed and leveled at its angle of inclination. Earth and gravel, millions of smaller stones, and the giant blocks of grey granite and syenite had to be brought to the site. The chief architect would probably have scratched his plans in ochre on reindeer skins and laid out angular measurements and string on the ground. In doing so, he kept scrupulously to the *megalithic yard*, the uniform unit of measurement in the Europe of the time discovered in our time by Professor Alexander Thom.[5] It corresponds precisely to 82.9 centimeters and spread from Newgrange to be used for all stone structures, be they in Stonehenge or Brittany in France. Presumably the Stone Age journal *Megalith Construction Today* was required reading.

If Newgrange (and other complexes) were conceived as graves, then the deceased person must have appeared to be superhuman to the society of that age. Why? At the birth of a child it could not be predicted whether he would become a hero or any other kind of "superman." But the construction of the grave, including all the preceding calculations, measurements, planning, and the cutting of the monoliths and the transport of the massive stones took at least one generation of the time. *Ergo* the father or grandfather would have had to commission the tomb for their future offspring. Whereby, they could not know whether he would become a hero at all and die in his home. He might just as well have died in battle far from his home tents and have been cremated elsewhere.

Here people will raise the objection—I can smell it coming— that these stone structures throughout the world with an astronomic reference performed a vital function as a calendar. This objection is of so little substance that I can hardly be bothered to deal with it again. What was the purpose of Newgrange? Was the place itself, the geographic location, a "sacred point"? Possibly, but then there has to be a surfeit of similar types of point. The world is drowning in megalithic complexes. Furthermore, the "sacred point" does not explain the astronomic and technical know-how.

The only thing that is actually certain is that someone in the mists of antiquity planted an astronomic precision timepiece into the landscape, a memorial which transmits its message with unaltered precision 5,000 (or more?) years later. What message? Who were these time thinkers, these initiates, who were able to impress both their time and the far distant future? And why did they do what they did? What was the trigger? What kind of person was at work here?

Farce

The progression from ape to intelligent human is a farce with thousands of open questions and thousands of incomplete answers. Every few years, the relevant science sells us the latest "assured knowledge" about the origin of species. The kind of pseudo-arguments which are used in textbooks to fill the gaping void in our knowledge is a sad sight to behold. I read, for example, that pre-hominids lived in packs and as a result developed intelligent and social behavior. Gruesome! Many animal species, not just apes, lived and live in packs. But apart from a hierarchy and pecking order, they have not developed any cultural intelligence. It is eternally argued that human beings are intelligent because they adapt better than other species. That objection is so much hot air. Why have other primates such as gorillas, chimpanzees, or orangutans not "adapted"? According to the rules of evolution, these cute animals would also have been "compelled" to develop intelligence. You cannot apply evolution selectively to one chosen species. The fact that we are intelligent really only says in comparison to the non-intelligent species that we should not be intelligent either. Furthermore, there are much older life forms than the primates. Scorpions, cockroaches, or spiders, for example, have been shown to have existed more than 500 million years in the past. The same applies to various species of reptiles, some of which are even said to have descended from the dinosaurs. Now we know that crocodile mothers care lovingly for their young, but crocodile culture is nevertheless lacking, despite all the millions of years in which they have "adapted." Because they all survived so bravely, these species should have squirmed through much better than the incomparably younger Homo sapiens. Where are the art objects or burial sites of these creatures?

When I read that humans do not have fur because they learned to cover themselves with other furs, I feel that someone is pulling my leg. The pre-hominids are said to have descended from the trees for climatic reasons. What a thought! As if an ape species had realized that in evolutionary theory, it might be needed for humans at some point in the future! It climbed down from the trees but left its compatriots—don't they imitate everything?—swinging from branch to branch in the trees to the present day. The social attitude of our ancestors left something to be desired.

The Trick With the Line

Nonsense, that is not how it was, there was something else, the clever articles say. Fear of stronger animals as well as easier nourishment had forced the pre-hominids to get up on their hind legs. What a laugh! The ape-like drive to imitate has become proverbial. Why did none of the other ape species follow this intelligent behavior? Were they less afraid of wild animals? And if such logic forced them to develop intelligence, then giraffes, who can see and smell any enemy from miles away, should really have developed a giraffe religion a long time ago. Finally, it is argued that all these changes only affect one particular line. The primates in our line had begun to eat meat to feed themselves better and more easily. As a result, our line achieved a significant advantage over other apes. Mama mia! Since when is it easier to kill a gazelle or salamander than pick fruits off a tree? Furthermore, wild cats or fish of prey have been eating meat for millennia, including the brain. Did they develop painting or mathematics as a result?

In a remarkable article in the specialist journal *Sagenhafte Zeiten*, the director of studies, Peter Fiebag, raises the question about the "human creative big bang": "Some experts believe a change in the 'wiring of the brain' had triggered the 'human creative big bang.'" And he adds, "A section of DNA was, by mistake, copied from the X chromosome to the Y chromosome."[6] Really, "by mistake," Fiebag asks? Or did it happen with the aid of extraterrestrial genetic engineering?

Fiebag's thought has a great deal of merit, even if anthropology has not quite caught up. There, in the salon of the sciences, we are served each year with the latest contradictions. Why not? Science is a living thing and the latest knowledge revises previous findings. Everyone is in agreement that we are unique. That also applies to other animals. But we are more unique than all the others because we have culture: painting, imagination, religion, mathematics, and the ability to plan for the future. (Though, the latter could be relativized, because a spider also plans for the future when it weaves its web.)

The lines of humans and chimpanzees had already been divided from before Eden, says Dr. David Reich from the Massachusetts Institute of Technology in Cambridge, Massachusetts. Then the two species had begun exchanging genes again: "After the pre-hominids had already lived as their own species for hundreds of thousands of years, they suddenly started to interbreed with their knuckle-walking relatives again."[7]

I have some difficulty with the idea of a hominid with an upright gait suddenly spurning the members of his own species and preferring to have sex with an ape lover. And why the resulting bastard should possess better genetic factors remains just as much of a riddle as the question of whether the chromosomes of the disparate pair would be compatible at all.

Things become even more confusing: mysterious bones were found in a cave in the Altai Mountains in central Asia, and analyzed at the Max Planck Institute for Evolutionary Anthropology in Leipzig: "The clearly human bone from the Denisova cave are not the same as the human genome. Sensationally the genetic material of the Denisova hominid differs from Homo sapiens by more than twice as much as from the Neanderthals."[8]

In the name of all that is Milky Way! Perhaps our venerable anthropology might dare to take a creative leap toward the Director of Studies Fiebag. It can be proved, after all, that the Stone Age people mastered the high art of mathematics and geometry and demonstrated it on site. Or do we all have to think differently? Do different types of humans perhaps exist alongside one another, the more stupid ones and the knowledgeable ones? The latter left examples of their skills, which are ignored by society to the present day, although any fool could verify them.

182

183

184

Poor Pythagoras!

Near the town of Carnac in Brittany, France, there are thousands of menhirs in long rows. (Images 182–185) Dr. Bruno P. Kremer from the Institute of Natural Science of the University of Cologne, who has published several papers on this arrangement of stones, estimates the number of menhirs still existing today as "more than 3,000."[9] And Pierre-Roland Giot, the leading expert on Brittany in France, is of the opinion that something approaching 10,000 menhirs must once have stood in the landscape.[10] Many of the granite blocks have been destroyed today, worn away by wind and weather. (Images 186–189) The ranks of three to 10 stones give the appearance of a petrified army. The smallest are barely 1 meter tall; the giant among them, the menhir of Kerloas near Plouarzel, is 12 meters high and weighs 150 tons. The largest "long stone" in the whole area is the menhir of Locmariaquer. It lies broken on the ground, was once

185

186

187

21 meters high, and weighed a good 350 tons. (Image 190) The most impressive thing is probably the long parallel columns of the Alignements (alignments). Near Kermario, there are 1,029 menhirs in 10 rows on an area about 100 meters wide and 1,120 meters long. At Ménec, there are 1,099 standing stones arranged in columns of 11. The Alignement of Kerlescan comprises 540 menhirs in rows of 13 and at Kerzehro we can count another 1,129 menhirs in columns of 10.

These are just some of the details, but they give an idea of the enormous work which was undertaken by someone at some stage. Carbon-14 dating at the dolmen of Kercado produced an age of 5,830 years. May the gods be thanked for this date, even if it might subsequently turn out to be too recent. At 5,830 years, all the nonsense put forward in all seriousness in the previous literature can at least be put to rest. It has been suggested, among other things,

EVIDENCE OF THE GODS

188

189

that primitive nomad tribes had cut and aligned stone blocks in European pre-history to copy the peoples of the East who possessed mighty structures in Egypt and elsewhere. Another current of thought suspects that the whole of the area which is Brittany today had once been sacred land of the Druids—but they reached their height in the last pre-Christian century. If therefore the Druids located their holy places in the network of menhirs, they must have taken over a complex that had already been finished and completed. It was originally believed that the stone columns were gravestones— but no bones ever materialized. Then someone thought it was a gigantic calendar in stone. Error. Even an astronomical alignment was assumed to be behind the long rows. In the meantime, we know better: they are about sophisticated geometry.

The western cromlech near Le Ménec includes two Pythagorean triangles whose sides have a ratio of 3:4:5. Pythagoras, the Greek philosopher from Samos, lived at about 532 BC. He cannot have

190

instructed the "nomad tribes and gatherers of berries" in his teachings. Poor Pythagoras! Your helpful theorems were already applied millennia before you.

If the trapeze-shaped sides are extended from the Manio I "warrior grave," they meet in an angle of 27 degrees at a distance of 107 meters. Exactly the same triangles with the same diagonals of 107 meters and the same side ratio of 5:12:13 occur several times in the stone settings of Carnac. Here it is surprising that the simple Pythagorean triangle with the classic ratio of 3:4:5 was seldom used. The megalithic people made use of higher geometry. In the journal *Naturwissenschaftliche Rundschau*,[11] Dr. Bruno Kremer points out that the individual ensembles were built in accordance with fixed "designated measures which allow us to conclude that highly developed surveying techniques existed as early as the Mesolithic period."

This involved not just applied geometry, but also the spherical shape of the earth, division into degrees, azimuth, organization, planning, transport of the stones, and many other things. Dr. Kremer refers to an angle of 53°8' which is based in a Pythagorean triangle with the ratio 3:4:5. The 53°8' corresponds "pretty precisely to the azimuth of the sunrise at the summer solstice *at all locations on the geographical latitude of Carnac.*"

The long stone columns of Le Ménec and Kermario run in a northeasterly direction and at their longest point touch the Alignement of Petit Ménec. This line is also the hypotenuse of a Pythagorean triangle. If we draw a line northward from the western end of the stone column of Le Ménec, it meets the dolmen of Mané Kérioned after 2,680 meters. From here, another line at exactly the same angle of 60 degrees heads for the menhir Manio I. *Once again the distance is 2,680 meters. The three points form an isosceles triangle; they are all equidistant.*

This is not some sort of arbitrary search for triangles. The points are connected in precisely the same distances at precisely the same angles. These large-scale examples can be endlessly repeated.

A north-south line runs from the eastern end of Le Ménec. In the south it touches the dolmen of St. Michel, in the north Le Nignol, and behind the village of Beg-Lann, the menhir Crucuny. The straight line lies within the triangle referred to previously, whereby Le Nignol marks exactly half the length. Another 60-degree angle produces an additional isosceles triangle with a side length of 1,680 meters: St. Michel–Le Nignol–Kercado. In doing so, the line Le Nignol–Kercado not only bisects the stone column of Kermario into two equally-sized sections, but the intersection simultaneously marks the halfway point of the hypotenuse of the Le Ménec–Petit Ménec route. As Dr. Kremer writes : "In view of the numerous relationships and alignments, there cannot reasonably be any further doubt that these megalithic complexes were planned in terms of their spatial organization."[12] (Images 191 and 192)

191

192

Questions No One Wants to Read

God did not set to work in Brittany, and we may exclude random chance altogether. What then, in the name of all the planets, were these Megalithic people about? What drove them? Where did their mathematical and geometric knowledge come from? What instruments did they use? What surveyors determined the fixed points in the uneven landscape? To what maps did they transfer their calculations? In what scale? With what string or, if you will, mirrors, did they communicate along the kilometer-long straight lines? How was the transport organized? What kinds of rope did they use—if any? How did the heavy transport function in winter? When it rained? When the ground was soft? What tools were used to cut the monolithic slabs? Why columns of menhirs of varying width and different rows? Sometimes nine, then 11 or 13 columns? What was the purpose of the stone ovals at the start and end of the Alignement at Le Ménec? How important was the way the space was divided, the smaller triangles within the larger ones? Why were stones of different sizes used? (Image 193) How much time was spent of planning before building began? What size was the workforce? Who directed the masses? Who had the supreme command and why? What legitimized the boss? Where did the workers and retinue sleep, spend the winter? Where are the remains of the resting places, their food, their bones? How long did the whole megalithic apparition last? If longer than one generation, what writing was used to pass on the instructions to the next generation?

The crazy thing is that it must all have happened in one generation, or else there must have been plans which were stubbornly adhered to over many generations. It is not possible to date Gavrinis, for example, at 4000 BC but to deny the same age to the large broken menhir or the dolmen of St. Pierre. Why not? All the points lie on one sight line. How were the megalithic people supposed to set a

193

sight on something that did not exist at the time? Consequently, the points were fixed at a specific time before building started.

As we can see, there are huge patches on the research map and no area that could be worked within one discipline alone.

Moral Courage in Demand

And what about "ley lines" or "geomancy"? These are straight lines that are from 150 to several thousand kilometers long and stretch like a grid across Europe. Never heard of them?

A straight line can be drawn on the map from Stonehenge, which lies northwest of Salisbury in England, to the Stone Age hill of Old Sarum. In its extension, this line runs directly over Salisbury Cathedral, Clearbury Ring, and Frankenbury Camp. All the places are prehistoric; Salisbury Cathedral was built on a heathen ceremonial site. Now stand on the top of Old Sarum and look northward and southward. A compass illustrates the straight sight line. All points can be seen from the top of the hill. There are masses of such lines and without exception they originate in the Stone Age. The journalist Paul Devereux, who specializes in archeology, and the mathematician Robert Forrest have critically studied these lines and end their contribution in the scientific journal *New Scientist* with the words: "There may be a modern unwillingness to admit that ancient societies once developed activities which we do not understand. That also applies with regard to the stubborn silence of archeology about the lines in the Peruvian Andes and equally to the stubborn resistance against a thorough investigation of ley lines in Europe."[13]

As long ago as 1870, William Henry Black (died 1872), a historian in the Public Record Office in London and member of the British Archeological Society, drew the attention of his colleagues to these curious lines: "The monuments, which we know about, mark great, geometrical lines. Lines which run across the whole of western Europe, across the British Isles and Ireland, the Hebrides, the Shetland and Orkney Islands as far as the Arctic Circle."[14]

One of these lines runs from Denmark right across the Alps and ends precisely on the ancient Greek sacred site of Delphi. Another starts at Calais in France, runs across Mont Alix, Mont Alet, L'Allet, Anxon, Aisey, Alaise, L'Alex, Alzano, etc. as far down as Sicily. All places on the route possess a Stone Age sacred site. And the name of each location has the same root—even today.

There is detailed literature about this phenomenon.[15, 16, 17, 18] Honest people have spent their lives researching these lines. People who were, of course, aware that the curvature of the earth had to be taken into account and who just as self-evidently knew that a straight line on a map will always randomly touch several locations. What remains is the facts, the "adjusted" points on a line. What do the opinionated critics care about that, who do not thoroughly

194

examine anything, yet *a priori* know everything better? One would have thought that the neat analysis of a prehistoric riddle would have contributed to the clarification of some truly exciting facts and would have made the specialist world prick up its ears. Mistake. The scientists in the field of primordial and pre-history are battening down the hatches and sticking their heads in the sand. They do not want to take account of what they think is impossible even if it is served to them on a plate. What has happened to the much-vaunted scientific thinking? Where is the drive of scientific discovery? Where is the pleasure in finding the truth?

I know what the problem is: a lack of moral courage. In Germany, no prehistoric specialist will tackle the subject because it might be connected with the "ancient Germanic peoples" and is thus automatically associated with Nazi thinking. And, in general, the ley lines lead to all kinds of impossible consequences. No maps and no writing are supposed to have existed thousands of years ago. How, then, can sight lines link Stone Age sacred sites over hundreds of kilometers in uneven terrain? Were they all constructed at the same time? If not, what was the obligation placed on succeeding generations? Generations which, like it or not, linked their later sacred sites in precise lines with the earlier sacred locations—whether or not that fitted with the spirit of the times. And who—one might well ask!—fixed the network of lines *before* the first building phase? That these lines from the Stone Age definitely exist is only disputed by those who do not want to know. Poor, dishonest society.

At least it is not disputed that, in Europe alone, there are several hundred prehistoric stone and wood circles. Mighty progress! That all these complexes are connected with astronomy is gradually also understood by most people. The blockade of reason starts when we ask "why?" *Why* did Stone Age people create magnificent, astronomically significant stone and wood circles?

In honor of those "heavenly teachers." That, at least, is the claim of the oldest account about the stone circle of Stonehenge.[19] (Image 194)

In ancient Egypt, the sun was given wings. But the winged sun disk, to be seen in all temples, also existed in ancient Babylon and still earlier among the Sumerians. Soon the divine kings had themselves immortalized with wings—they can be found in any larger museum today. The Christians turned these flying figures into angels. The angel (*angelos*) was a messenger, a mediator between the world of the gods and of humans—hence the wings. And we also brought along from antiquity the helmets—pardon me, the haloes—of those untouchable beings in the pictorial images.

The world of our imagination has changed little over millennia—apart from psychology explaining many things in the wrong way.

References

Islands in the Pacific

1. Rittlinger, Herbert. *Der masslose Ozean: Roman d. Südsee.* Stuttgart: Stuttgarter Hausbücherei, 1957.

2. Hambruch, Paul. *Ponape, Ergebnisse der Südsee-Expedition.* Berlin: 1936.

3. Ibid.

4. Buchmüller, Gottfried. *St. Beatenberg: Geschichte einer Berggemeinde.* Bern: Wyss, 1914.

5. Danielsson, B. *Vergessene Inseln der Südsee.* Frankfurt: 1955

6. White, John. *Ancient History of the Maori*, Volume I–III. Wellington, New Zealand: Government Printer, 1887.

7. Ibid.

8. Brugsch, Heinrich. *Die Sage von der geflügelten Sonnenscheibe nach altägyptischen Quellen.* Göttingen: In der Dieterichschen Buchhandlung, 1870.

9. Buck, Peter H. *Vikings of the Pacific.* Chicago [u.a.]: Univ. of Chicago Press, 1972.

10. Handy, Edward Smith Craighill. *The Native Culture in the Marquesas.* Honolulu : Bernice P. Bishop Museum, Bulletin Nr. 9, 1923.

11. Handy, Edward Smith Craighill. *Polynesian Religion.* Honolulu : Bishop Museum Bulletin, Nr. 34, 1927.

12. Andersen, Johannes Carl, and Richard Wallwork. *Myths & Legends of the Polynesians.* Rutland, Vt: C.E. Tuttle Co, 1969.

13. *Die Heilige Schrift des Alten und des Neuen Testaments.* Stuttgart :Württembergische Bibelanstalt, 1972.

14. Fox, Charles Elliot, Grafton Elliot Smith, and Frederic Henry Drew. *The Threshold of the Pacific.* London: K. Paul, Trench, Trubner & Co, 1924.

15. Kohlenberg, Karl, F. *Enträtselte Vorzeit.* Munich: 1970.

16. Talu, Alaima, et. al. *Kiribati: Aspects of History.* Tarawa: Ministry of Education, Training and Culture, 1979.

17. Grimble, Arthur. *A Pattern of Islands.* London: Murray, 1970.

18. Turbott, I.G. "The Footprints of Tarawa." *Journal of the Polynesian Society*, Extract from Vol.58 No.4. December 1949. Wellington, New Zealand.

19. Aitken, Robert T. *Ethnology of Tubuai.* Honolulu, Hawaii: Bernice P. Bishop Museum, 1930.

20. White, John. *Ancient History of the Maori*, Volume I. Wellington, New Zealand: Government Printer, 1887.

21. Heyerdahl, T. *Aku-Aku.* Munich: 1957.

22. Langbein, Walter-Jörg. *Die großen Rätsel der letzten 2500 Jahre: seltsame Ereignisse aus 2500 Jahren.* Augsburg: Weltbild-Verl, 1992.

23. Degen, Rolf. "Schufen Germanen die Wunder der Osterinsel?" *Neue Zürcher Zeitung*, Zürich: October 31, 1984.

Saluting the Gods

1. Tobisch, Oswald Oskar. *Kult-Symbol-Schrift.* Baden-Baden: Verlag für angewandte Wissenschaften, 1963.

2. Pager, Harald. *Ndedema: A Documentation of the Rock Paintings of the Ndedema Gorge.* Graz: 1971.

3. Weber, Gertrud, and Matthias Strecker. *Petroglyphen der Finca Las Palmas* (Chiapas, Mexico). Graz, Austria: Akademische Druck- und Verlagsanstalt, 1980.

4. Uyanik, Muvaffak. *Petroglyphs of South-Eastern Anatolia.* Graz: Akadem. Druck- u. Verlagsanst, 1974.

5. Noack, Herbert, Sigrid Ortner, and Dieter Ortner. *Felsbilder der spanischen Sahara.* Graz: Akademische Druck- u. Verlagsanstalt, 1975.

6. Weaver, Donald E. *Images on Stone: The Prehistoric Rock Art of the Colorado Plateau.* Flagstaff, Ariz: Museum of Northern Arizona, 1984.

7. Jettmar, Karl, and Volker Thewalt. *Zwischen Gandhara und den Seidenstrassen: Felsbilder am Karakorum Highway: Entdeckungen deutsch-pakistanischer Expeditionen, 1979-84.* Mainz am Rhein: Von Zabern, 1985.

8. Cox, J. Halley, and Edward Stasack. *Hawaiian Petroglyphs.* Honolulu, Hawaii: Bishop Museum Press, 1970.

9. Biedermann, Hans. *Bildsymbole der Vorzeit: Wege zur Sinndeutung der schriftlosen Kulturen.* Graz: Verlag für Sammler, 1977.

10. Priuli, Ausilio. *Felszeichnungen in den Alpen.* Zürich: Benziger, 1984.

11. Lhote, Henri. *Die Felsbilder der Sahara, Entdeckung einer 8000 jährigen Kultur.* Würzburg: A. Zettner, 1963.

12. Blumrich, J. F. *Kásskara und die sieben Welten: Weisser Bär erzählt den Erdmythos der Hopi-Indianer.* Wien: Econ, 1979.

13. Waters, Frank, and Oswald White Bear Fredericks. *Book of the Hopi.* New York: Viking Press, 1963.

14. Schwennhagen, Ludwig, and Moacir C. Lopes. *Antiga história do Brasil*. Rio de Janeiro: Livraria e Editôra Cátedra, 1970.

15. Däniken, Erich von. *Zeichen für die Ewigkeit die Botschaft von Nazca*. Munich: Bertelsmann, 1997.

16. Coe, Michael, D. *Die Nazca-Scharrbilder*. Munich: 1986.

17. Isbell, William, H. "Die Bodenzeichnungen Altperus." *Spektrum der Wissenschaften*, December 1978.

18. Tributsch, Helmut. *Das Rätsel der Götter: Fata Morgana*. Frankfurt/Main u.a: Ullstein, 1983.

19. Gentes, Lutz. *Die Wirklichkeit der Götter: Raumfahrt im frühen Indien*. Munich; Essen ; Ebene Reichenau: Bettendorf, 1996.

20. Kanjilal, Dileep Kumar. *Vimana in Ancient India*. Calcutta: Sanskrit Pustak Bhandar, 1985.

21. Kautzsch, E., and Georg Beer. *Die Apokryphen und Pseudepigraphen des Alten Testaments*. Tübingen, Freiburg i.B. [etc.]: Mohr, 1900.

22. *Kebra Nagast*, Vol 23, Section 1: "The Glory of the Kings." Treatise of the philosophical and philological class of the Royal Bavarian Academy of Sciences.

23. Mas'udi, and Gernot Rotter. *Bis zu den Grenzen der Erde: Ausz. aus d. Buch der Goldwäschen*. Tübingen: Erdmann, 1978.

24. Kanjilal, Dileep Kumar. *Vimana in Ancient India*. Calcutta: Sanskrit Pustak Bhandar, 1985.

25. Bopp, Franz. *Ardschuna's Reise zu Indra's Himmel: nebst anderen Episoden des Maha-bharata*. Berlin: Königl. Akademie der Wissenschaften, 1824.

26. Vyasa, Kisari Mohan Ganguli, Protap Chandra Roy, and Sundari Bala Roy. *The Mahabharata of Krishna-Dwaipayana Vyasa*. Calcutta: Bharata Press, 1889.

Stones Can Talk

1. Le Scouëzec, Gwenc'hlan, and Jean-Robert Masson. *Bretagne mégalitique*. Paris: Seuil, 1987.

2. Ibid.

3. O'Kelly, M. Newgrange. London: 1983.

4. Ray, I.P. "The Winter Solstice at New Grange, Ireland. Accident or Design?" *Nature*, January 1989, Vol. 337.

5. Thom, Alexander. *Megalithic Sites in Britain*. Oxford: Clarendon Pr, 1967.

6. Fiebag, Peter. "Der kreative Urknall des Menschen." *Sagenhafte Zeiten*, Volume 12, No. 2/2010.

7. *Der Spiegel* No. 21/2006.

8. Kulke, Ulli. "Der neue Nachbar aus der Höhle." *Die Welt Am Sonntag*, No. 13. March 28, 2010.

9. Kremer, Bruno, P. "Geometrie in Stein." *Antike Welt*, Volume 18, Issue 1, 1987.

10. Kremer, Bruno, P. "Mass und Zahl in den Megalithdenkmälern der Bretagne." *Naturwissenschaftliche Rundschau*, Volume 37, Issue 12, 1984.

11. Ibid.

12. Kremer, Bruno, P. "Geometrie in Stein."

13. Devereux, Paul, and Robert Forrest. "Straight Lines on Ancient Landscape." *New Scientist*, 30 December 30, 1982.

14. Pennick, Nigel. *Die alte Wissenschaft der Geomantie*. Munich: Trikont-dianus, 1982.

15. Pennick, Nigel, and Soni Arnoldt. *Einst war uns die Erde heilig: die Lehre von den Erdkräften und Erdstrahlen.* Zürich: Oesch, Abt. Hübner, 1987.

16. Heinsch, Josef. Grundsätze vorzeitlichen *Kultgeographie.* Moers: 1947.

17. Fester, Richard. *Protokolle der Steinzeit.* Munich: Herbig, 1974.

18. Fester, Richard. *Die Steinzeit liegt vor deiner Tür: Ausflüge in die Vergangenheit.* Munich: Kösel-Verlag, 1981.

19. Jones, Inigo, and Graham Parry. *The Most Notable Antiquity of Great Britain Vulgarly Called Stonehenge 1655.* Reprinted in London 1973.

Index

About the Author

Born on April 14th, 1935, in Zofingen, Switzerland, Erich von Däniken was educated at the College St. Michel in Fribourg, where he was already occupying his time with the study of ancient holy writings. While managing director of a Swiss 5-star hotel, he wrote his first book, *Chariots of the Gods*, which was an immediate best-seller in the United States, Germany, and later in 38 other countries. He won instant fame in the United States as a result of the television special *In Search of Ancient Astronauts*, which was based on that book. His other books, including the more recent *Twilight of the Gods* and *Odyssey of the Gods*, have been translated into 32 languages and have sold more than 63 million copies worldwide.

From his books, two full-length documentary films have been produced, *Chariots of the Gods* and *Messages of the Gods*. As well, the History Channel is continuing its extremely successful series *Ancient Aliens*, for which Giorgio A. Tsoukalos, of the Center for Ancient Astronaut Research and publisher of *Legendary Times* magazine, serves as consulting producer.

Of the more than 3,000 lectures that Erich von Däniken has given in 25 countries, more than 500 were presented at universities. Fluent in four languages, Erich von Däniken is an avid researcher and a compulsive traveler, averaging 100,000 miles each year to the most remote spots on the globe. This enables him to closely examine the phenomena about which he writes. Erich von Däniken is a member of the Swiss Writers Association, the German Writers Association, and the International PEN Club. He was awarded with an honorary doctorate degree by the La Universidad Boliviana. He received the Huesped Illustre award from the cities of Ica and Nazca in Peru. In Brazil he received the Lourenço Filho award in Gold and Platinum, and in Germany he was awarded with the Order of Cordon Bleu du Saint Esprit (together with the German astronaut Ulf Merbold). In 2004, he was awarded the Explorers Festival prize.

In 1998, Erich von Däniken cofounded the Archaeology, Astronautics, and SETI Research Society (AASRS), which publishes the English journal *Legendary Times*, reporting on the latest research in the paleo-SETI field. In 2003, he opened his "Mysteries of the World" theme park in Interlaken, Switzerland, which still fascinates visitors with his research into the various mysteries of the world, including paleo-SETI and the Ancient Astronaut Theory.

Today, Erich von Däniken lives in the small mountain village of Beatenberg in Switzerland (40 miles from Berne, above the city of Interlaken). He has been married to Elisabeth Skaja since 1960. He has one daughter, Cornelia (born 1963), and two grandchildren. Von Däniken is an amateur chef and a lover of Bordeaux wines.

Other Titles From
NEW PAGE BOOKS

EAN 978-1-60163-232-6   EAN 978-1-60163-198-5   EAN 978-1-60163-207-4

Featuring Work by **Erich von Däniken**

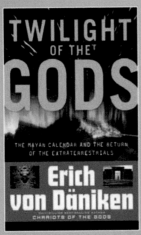

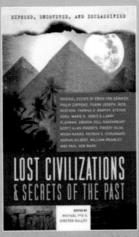

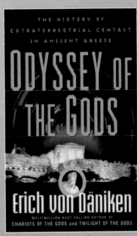

EAN 978-1-60163-141-1   EAN 978-1-60163-196-1   EAN 978-1-60163-192-3